Waves of
Change

Waves of Change

GROWTH MINDSET TOOLS FOR CONNECTED BALANCE

KATHRYN SEBUCK

WAVES OF CHANGE
Growth Mindset Tools for Connected Balance

Published through IngramSpark

PRINT ISBN: 979-8-9855051-0-8

EBOOK ISBN: 979-8-9855051-1-5

Acknowledgements

To my family and everyone on my path,
thank you for your support and the opportunity to learn.

To my tribe, I am eternally grateful for you and all the laughs.

Special thanks to Holly Hudson, Tanya MacIntosh,
Monica Hickey, and Twig Interactive
for your **outstanding** services.

This book is dedicated to my Father, who is now
a COVID-19 statistic. RIP Coach Sebuck.

About the Author

A Chicago native, Kathy is a midwestern girl at heart with a wanderlust for travel. She successfully outran Old Man Winter in late 2020, and now lives near the beaches of Southern California - once a dream, now a reality. A secret mermaid, she always wanted to live somewhere warm near the water and be active outside year-round, not freeze to death half the year. Winter PTSD is very real for some, just ask anyone from Chicago. She is a strategic thinker, entrepreneurial leader, athlete, and author with over 25 years of IT sales and marketing leadership expertise. She worked for tech startups and Fortune 500 enterprise software companies in the public and private sectors including Sun Microsystems, Verisign, Citrix, Microsoft, and SAP. Today, she provides strategic marketing consulting services, is a mentor for entrepreneurial incubator programs, and teaches marcom strategy and storytelling workshops to educate and drive business growth. Kathy holds a BS in Public Relations from Illinois State University, an MS in Management from Southern Nazarene University, and a Digital Marketing Professional certification from the Digital Marketing Institute in Dublin, Ireland. For more information, visit www.marchitecturemarketing.com.

Prologue

"There's no secret to balance,
you just have to feel the waves."

~ Frank Herbert

A
s the COVID-19 pandemic shut down the world in Spring 2020, I celebrated a milestone birthday one afternoon in my garage. My golf crew created a surprise parade of "crazy" down my block from the safety of their cars. We have been playing a different kind of golf game for years across many states and countries, always focused on fun with no limits. From wearing costumes and props to sand trap marching, playing pig dice, animal headcover hide and seek, stick horse prancing, and cartwheels for big putts, we always enjoy our round since having fun is our goal. While we've won a few tournaments, drive contests, closest to the pin, and a couple of holes in one, the games we play are more reindeer

related and just the way I like to roll - with belly laughs like teenagers because life is short.

These festivities were followed up later that evening with a socially distanced surprise birthday party in a Grand Hyatt lobby hosted by the "Go Club." The GC is always ready to "go" on a new adventure and has been traveling the globe together for almost two decades, sometimes in matching t-shirts and with a pinata in tow. Since most people were sheltering in place and there was minimal risk to the hotel and to us, the hotel staff allowed this little soiree to take place on a Thursday night in April. This is when having premiere hotel status comes in handy. My celebration had cocktails, food, cupcakes, and the standard "wet-your-pants" laughs. For one night, we were able to forget that the world was slowly melting down into a dark abyss. We created priceless memories just like a Mastercard commercial. To say that I am grateful for **all** my girlfriends is an understatement: I know not everyone has the connections they need in their life or the precious laughs to be able to let go or feel accepted, loved, and supported.

Months later as I looked back on those amazing memories, the idea for this book sparked into a flame in my imagination.

People say that a crisis or a milestone event can cause a person to stop, reflect, and make big life changes. I know this is true because I have experienced both and too many to count. These camouflaged growth opportunities have reinforced the importance of my connections to my family and friends, my relationships, accomplishments, and failures. They are reminders of how thankful I am for the tools I have learned from many on my path as I continue to navigate the changing tide of life. My gratitude and growth extends across and interconnects with so many amazing people: the alternative healers I work with to support my health and wellbeing; my long-lost brother in San Diego; my triathlon coach and dear friend who taught me there is more to life than racing; my girlfriends who laugh at and with me; my bosses who believed I could; the people on my teams who trust my skills; and my colleagues who support me. Thank you!

I believe having supportive people around you throughout your life is half the battle: they help keep you grounded when life blows up and help you celebrate everything that matters. While this is not something new, the tools you pick up along the way become staples for better navigation on the high seas. During this last year, I reconfirmed for myself how important the people in my life are and decided that anyone can benefit from new tools. I wrote this book to provide others with the same opportunity to learn, should they choose to explore as I did. I hope you find something of value here that helps you on your path. Anything good is worth sharing.

Table of Contents

Introduction

"Courage is what it takes to stand up
and speak; Courage is also what
it takes to sit down and listen."

~ Winston Churchill

was a busy child, a curious learner that loved to sing, dance, and laugh. I was always full of endless energy. I looked for any chance to play outside that blew off steam, running around with the neighborhood kids. My parents knew first-hand that the more energy I ran off outside, the better I would sleep – God bless them. It was my running around that made me feel alive and free, whether I was running down the block chasing someone playing flashlight tag or riding my bike ped-aling as fast as I could to be the first one down the hill back to our driveway. Ready, set, go! I was always up for the challenge with anyone who wanted to take me on. Ready to play no mat-ter what the game or who was playing. I believe that love of being outside and running led to a collegiate track career.

My Dad has been coaching high school football for over 50 years, so growing up in a house around competitive sports, I picked up a passion for competition. Determined to win at all costs no matter what the game, I felt most alive when I could hear my heart pounding in my ears and feel it beating like a drum in my chest as the beads of sweat streamed down my back. That was living in my book and the early start of my life-long need for that adrenaline fix.

It's no wonder I spent most of my life living in extremes while I ran my body into the ground through sports to feel better about myself. Instead of learning about self-care and how to love myself for the amazing person I was, I often judged my self-worth and everything in my life by the sports I played, my fitness level, winning, and losing. The silver lining is I did pick up my parents' strong work ethic among other great traits like unconditional love and support. That trans-lated into becoming a successful team player in various sports and later created the invisible bridge to a successful career. Unfortunately, that did not transfer well into my personal life, the place where I would learn my most difficult life lessons.

I've spent the first half of my life using sports as a tool to manage stress, to find peace, and to learn. From playing three sports in high school to running indoor and outdoor track at a Division I university, and now as a sprint triathlete after 20 years of competitive age-group racing, I discovered that fitness benefits are positive when they are balanced. When left unchecked, however, the body takes the brunt of that beating and eventually shuts down, offering a sharp reminder of ignored emotional pain. Add into the mix my type A+ personality and get-it-done mentality, I ended up driving unrealistic expectations around goals and successful outcomes.

Drive is a great trait since a strong work ethic is required to reach any level of achievement. It is this type of driven mindset, though, that opened the door for years of crash-and-burn behavior patterns from my subconscious. I've worked hard, I've struggled, and I've been fortunate to reap the rewards of all that hard work, but it didn't come without a price. With a successful career, financial security, a collection of triathlon medals, trophies, and plaques plus the trauma of divorce all under my belt before age 40, I was exhausted. I started to become painfully aware of the impact and the cumulative cost of my lack of personal tools and coping skills.

Over time, I had slowly shut down emotionally and had become disconnected from myself, my feelings, my needs. I started to recognize that I was attracting the same disconnection into my life. Can you say butterfly effect? It is amazing how the mind will settle back into old familiar patterns in the blink of an eye, repeating the same crash-and-burn behavior, regardless of the cost. I felt like my scorecard included more personal losses than wins which was not where I expected to find myself. It was like I woke up one day, looked in the mirror and said, "Who are you and what have you done with my happy place?" I was living but asleep, operating on autopilot, listening to the same bad subconscious tape replaying itself over and over screaming, "You don't deserve to be happy!"

Some call this voice *the roommate in your head*, some call it *the ego*. Others aren't sure what to make of it even though we all have experienced it. One thing is certain: those who choose to be emotionally aware know that this voice should be ignored at all costs because it just generates a lot of negative self-talk. This kind of energy doesn't come from a place of self-love. Instead, it feeds on fear, uncertainty, and doubt. It was time for me to make a new choice: go inside and listen to my true inner voice, not the crazy roommate in my head who thinks she has all the answers. I was finally awake, present, conscious, and in control of my own life, my own path, and my own decisions.

As I continue to detach from old beliefs that no longer serve me, I now have a heightened awareness that often reminds me to step away from the fear narrative that will stop any of us dead in our tracks. I have learned through various people, books, and practices how to become the observer of my past, my thoughts, and, especially, of the things that unfold in my life to help create a stronger sense of grounded balance. Now, I'm not suggesting everyone should look for a mid-life crisis, create an illness, or expect to have some sort of awakening moment to find her soul. I've just found over the years to stop looking to others for fulfillment, connection, stability, and love. Instead, I'm learning to look within and focus on personal happiness that can be generated by living life in the present moment. A life that I create and own is the true answer to cracking life's Da Vinci code. As I peel my own healing onion layer by layer, I've come to understand more about my boundaries, my needs, and why my crash-and-burn patterns were repeating. My past baggage that I was dragging behind me like a boat anchor and my outdated belief system was absolutely killing my soul. It was time to let all that go, write a new story, and begin a different journey focused on connection, forgiveness, love. It was time for me to stop subconsciously blaming others for my unhappiness.

I began to really look at my thoughts and my overall well-being with a critical eye. As my body had taken the brunt of all my stuffed emotions and "busy" stress over the years, it was now fighting back in full-assault mode due to the cumulative cost. My body was sending me loud, very strong messages that it was time to make some changes. I had no choice but to listen or I would eventually end up in the hospital or worse, I would exit this life. Once I stopped looking outside myself to get my needs met, it became very clear to me of the ongoing work I needed to do, that inside work many of us do as adults, whether we want to or not. Tending to your garden if you will. I now set aside regular time to quietly connect with myself and just listen. Call it meditation, call it a break, call it a workout or an escape. Regardless of the label, I have found this necessary to keep grounded during today's technology-driven rat race we call life. Instead of ignoring my gut instincts when things don't feel right, I stop, take a breath, and see what I can hear or feel. It is in this stillness that I have been able to find the peace and the answers I need to guide my life, my journey, and my purpose.

Everyone knows life is short, many believe it, but most don't take this little statement to heart usually until after something bad or catastrophic happens and that wakeup call arrives. How we choose to answer that call is up to us; however, if we don't, the other side of that equation is usually big regret. I never really understood the timeless adage that with age comes wisdom until now. I understand the gravity of the fact that the amount of time we have here on earth is finite and that our hopes, dreams, and plans have a shelf life. Add a life crisis into the mix, a pandemic, or the death of a loved one and that creates more sensitivity and awareness around where we are in our lives, who we spend our time with, and what we hope to accomplish personally and professionally.

This book is for anyone who has ever found themselves in this position wondering: how did I get here? Or, is this it? It is for those who are open-minded and want connected balance in their life, some new tools for personal clarity, better stress management, and a few laughs to keep it real. The goal is to take ownership for how you live and manage your life and be less tethered to that idea of someone else's making – whether a parent, a spouse, or society. It is a resource to help you reclaim your personal power, to find the connection and balance you crave, to bring joy every day at work and at home. This compendium offers ancient wisdom, historical tested concepts, business insight, and innovative ideas all wrapped up in storytelling to help you find your voice, write your own story, live your best life, and trust that the Universe has your back. Carpe Diem!

Chapter One

Incoherence

"That which does not kill us
makes us stronger."

~ Friedrich Nietzsche

t is the morning of my 40th birthday. I am sitting alone shivering in a paper-thin gown on the exam table. My mind is racing while I wait for the test results. When the fertility doctor reappears, his face is arranged in that steely I-have-bad-news-for-you kind of way that only a medical professional can deliver.

"You've tested positive for ovarian cancer," he says.

A knot forms in my stomach. My heart begins to pound as if I might go into cardiac arrest right there on the table. Then, after the initial moment of shock subsides, I snap, "I'm sorry, what did you just say?" with squinted eyes. This death sentence is not my idea of the best way to celebrate my milestone birthday especially since no cocktail was offered.

I become impatient with his silence, lean towards him in attack mode, and challenge his announcement with a barrage of questions.

"How is this possible with no symptoms? Which test points to that diagnosis? How often is this test a false positive? I don't have cancer!" I shout in rambling disbelief. How could a person have cancer and not have one single symptom? I can't wrap my head around it logically, so I choose to dismiss it regardless of the fact that ovarian cancer is a silent killer. I don't want to shoot the messenger, though, so I quickly get myself under control, get dressed, and start walking towards the door.

He begins again, "Your numbers are abnormally high for the C125 blood test marker, a standard indicator of cancer. Your best option is a referral we can provide to an OB/GYN oncology practice for additional testing." I am two steps away from losing all rational thought when I take a deep breath, cut him off, and say, "Thanks for your time," walk out and head back to work.

Later at home that evening, I fumble around the kitchen, trying to figure out how to break the news to my husband. He yells over from where he's sitting in front of the TV, "How did your tests go today?"

I feel my irritation quickly heat up from hot-tea-kettle status to what is threatening to become a raging late-night bonfire in my gut. I'm already disappointed that he couldn't find the time to attend this critical medical appointment - especially on my birthday – and now, his laissez-faire demeanor pushes me over the edge. Ironically, he hasn't hesitated to tell me on more than one occasion in jest that I'm the reason our pregnancy plans were failing. Some joke, huh? That's not my idea of funny, especially since the punchline falls flat.

"Apparently, I have ovarian cancer. How's that for a birthday present?" I yell back.

He seems unfazed by this announcement and looks at me blankly. "So, what are you going to do now?" He turns his gaze back towards the TV. The conversation resembles something you experience in a grocery store checkout line where strangers exchange pleasantries that are as impersonal as preparing for severe weather and stockpiling necessities. Can you say toilet paper, anyone?

At this point, the wheels on the bus of my life started to come off one at a time, and that bus was careening in DUI-like fashion. As it turns out, the oncology diagnosis that followed was quite different. While thankfully the issue was not ovarian cancer, over the next seven years a series of reproductive surgeries would be needed to address this problem which sadly affects 10 percent of women.

The diagnosis brought to light how unsustainable my life had become. Somehow, somewhere along the way, I got lost in the noise and the shuffle of it all. I was running myself ragged trying to keep up with a 24/7 career, and in a dead-end marriage that ended with the admission of my husband's infidelity. I later thanked God that I had dodged a bullet by not being able to conceive, given this marriage was doomed to fail for obvious reasons. The experience was Divine intervention. The Universe had my back and this was one of those defining moments in life that was excruciatingly painful at the time, yet later turns out to be a huge gift. It was time to learn how to manage my lack of balance and address the toxic environment I was living in that created high levels of stress and physical health issues.

When I think about how many people fly on autopilot through life dialed into "busy" mode, I am reminded of the legend of the musk deer. I can't remember where I originally heard the story from, but it has always stuck with me. It goes something like this:

One day, the male musk deer sniffed the most intoxicating whiff of musk perfume. Intrigued by this scent, he followed it as best he could over the rocky mountains, down into ravines, through forests, over hills and under brambles. He spent his life chasing this scent. Finally, exhausted and starving, he slipped from atop a rock and tumbled down the mountainside. As he lay there dying, he licked a wound on his belly. This was his musk pouch, torn open by the fall after being snagged on a rock. The scent he had been searching for emanated from his belly and he died, finally finding the object of all his journeys – the scent which was within him all along.

Sound tragic? It absolutely is since so many of us live this way. At some point in our lives, we are all searching for something that makes us feel better and that we usually think is outside of ourselves. If only that deer knew that it really was an inside job. As you've probably guessed by now, the lesson of this apocryphal tale is that what you seek is with you all along. The truth is you can interpret it in a number of ways. I like to think that the message is: your own truth has always been with you if you would just wake up and smell the coffee! or the tea! or the musk!

These are interesting times we are living in. I am, by nature, an optimist who loves to laugh, and I honestly believe it is an amazing time to be alive on planet Earth if you can look past the current car accident in front of you. There are more opportunities now than at any time in human history for people to create lives filled with both meaning and economic viability. The vast spread of innovative technology and internet access enables more people to work remotely with the means to make a sustainable living, no matter where they are in the world, whether they live in Peoria or Phuket. At the same time, our world faces unprecedented challenges. The climate is getting hotter every year, fires continue to blaze, and we face global climate changing events on a scale never seen before. Civil unrest and access to the most basic human rights, whether it is the right to speak freely or consume clean water and electricity, still elude many populations across the globe.

We have the collective intelligence, creativity, and moral compass to create change and make the world a welcoming, kind, and a great place to live – if we put our heads together and work across political and international lines on these most fundamental problems. Closer to home in America, I have noticed another crisis of sorts going on amongst the working class across all kinds of industries, from finance to tech, from entrepreneurs to solopreneurs. I call this crisis Zuckerbergitis. Driven by greed, it is an affliction whereby people have become irrationally obsessed with becoming the next Facebook-type startup and, in the process, have lost sight of the forest for the trees. Or to put it more simply, they have lost sight of their own inner truth, their own intoxicating scent, in the pursuit of the myth of cashing out on the American dream.

I call it a myth because by now there is plenty of evidence to suggest that the American "business" dream that we were all fed growing up in the 20th century is not available to everyone. Why else would we currently be living in such a visibly divided country, the likes of which have never been seen this starkly at any other time in history? The reason I titled this chapter Incoherence is because I believe there is a profound lack of alignment and balance in our approach to work and life due to our gold-ring money chasing culture. Remember when you were small, and you saw the merry-go-round ride at the amusement park with the wooden horses that went up and down? On some of those rides, there was a gold ring you could reach for each time your horse passed it. But it always seemed to be too far away. I could swear the ride operators were moving it. And you had to be careful in case you reached too far and fell off that damned wooden horse!

I can call the kettle black, so to speak, because I have been guilty of this myself. In fact, I lived it. Several years ago, my career was flying like a rocket ship on steroids. I was traveling internationally nonstop. City-hopping from one conference, meeting, or assignment to the next, airport lounges and hotel rooms were my usual stomping ground. I survived on massive amounts of post-workout adrenalin in the mornings or after lunch to get me through the day, then sprinted to business happy hours with the gusto of a quarterback running toward the end zone to show off her dance moves. Given the apple never falls far from the tree, if I had learned one thing from my father growing up in the "winners never quit" circle, it was go hard or go home. That was my motto, which I had perfected from watching the expert coach football for decades. Until I got sick.

As I mentioned, I finally got the message loud and clear and knew I needed more balance in my life – the question was how. I realized I could not keep up this pace, though the culture all around me had no problem encouraging me to keep-on-keeping-on. There is always a to-do list waiting some-where. Learning better boundaries and how to effectively use the word "no" became a survival must. I was painfully aware something needed to change - and that something was me.

We all find ways to get through life's personal and profes-sional challenges. There are several types of maladaptive cop-ing behavior that many of us use, from exercise and alcohol to drugs, food, sex, online shopping, workaholism and countless other types of addictive and destructive behaviors. I was no different. Like the time in college, I decided it was a good idea to keep pushing my body when I knew something wasn't right and I felt off, but I continued to train and race, assuming it would pass. "Run through the pain." I was taught in college that injuries didn't matter, we still needed to win that meet at all costs. It was as if life and death was decided on a collegiate track like an emergency room doctor assessing a car accident victim in grave condition. In my professional life, I was pulling all-nighters to meet project deadlines, watching that pattern continue as unrealistic job expectations were set and bars were raised because, "We have revenue goals to meet!" I do not believe life is supposed to be run like an ER triage room and I challenge anyone who does, other than the ER doctors who work in one.

My stories are not uncommon, but my actions following them usually are. Learning to manage life's emotional pain and changing behaviors, patterns, and beliefs is a hero's journey that many ignore; the alternative, I believe, is worse. Western corporate culture has been my playground for the past three decades. Anyone familiar with this paradigm knows that no matter what lip service may be given to work-life balance, it is still, well into the 21st century, a take-no-prisoners workplace climate where working 60–80-hour weeks was more the norm, a badge of honor, and usually rewarded. Until, of course, the pandemic changed all the rules. The mere idea that American business might one day mirror the culture in Finland, or other parts of Europe where new mothers and fathers can take six months to a year of paid maternity and paternity leave or where workers regularly enjoy 3-4 weeks of paid holiday annually, is unheard of in the U.S. America is getting better at creating a new perceived normal that provides the needed time off from a job to live life and for better mental health, but we still have a long way to go.

People can say this is the trade-off we make for being Number One in the world. What is it that we really want to be known as Number One for? It seems the areas we currently are leading in are heart disease, obesity, depression, and teenage pregnancy. Yikes.

As I write this book, we are still navigating our fluid post-pandemic culture and there are many things left to shake out just like during the Spanish Flu in 1918 when the future was uncertain. Is the future ever certain? Isn't that the reason it's the future? A question for Michael J. Fox, maybe? The new work-from-home Zoom culture that developed, by necessity, has called into question the long-perceived requirement that we need to be tethered to a shared cube farm in a fluorescent lit drop-ceiling room to perform at our jobs. Companies have found their employees to be just as efficient, if not more so working remotely, leaving many to rethink the expensive overhead costs for maintaining leases on office spaces now rendered pointless.

According to a recent Wall Street Journal article, before the pandemic, only approximately 10 percent of the U.S. workforce worked remotely. As of March 2021, as much as a quarter of the 160 million people in the U.S. workforce is expected to remain fully remote in the long term.[1] The Journal reports that

---

[1] Florida and Ozimek. (2021). https://www.wsj.com/articles/how-remote-work-is-reshaping-americas-urban-geography-11614960100

the productivity boost from remote workers is as high as 2.5 percent. The way we are working has shifted, which I believe is a step in the right direction. The fundamental mindset we are working with unfortunately has not.

The American Dream persists and infuses every aspect of our workplace and cultural life. It is the reason that many still try emigrating to America to build a business and become the next billionaire. What I call the myth of the American Dream persists because it is like an urban legend, passed around until it is blithely accepted as fact – that if a person works hard enough, no matter how low their economic status is, they can achieve middle class status, or higher. It is very ironic that, in fact, it is actually harder to advance in America than it is in other nations. According to research from University of Ottawa economist Miles Corak, only the United Kingdom and Italy have less upward economic mobility than America and many other nations score better than the U.S. like Germany, Scandinavia, Australia, and Japan.[2]

There is a cycle of poverty that is as endemic to America as the favelas, or shanty towns, are to Rio de Janeiro. Corak's research also suggests that having a stable homelife is a notable factor in being able to climb the economic ladder and the U.S. has higher rates of divorce, single parent homes, and teenage pregnancy than other industrialized countries. Again, ironic that the traits as Americans we love to celebrate – individuality, hard work, persistence – make it more difficult as a society to be connected and functional. A country that does not embrace social policies such as higher taxes on the

---

[2] Hargreaves. (2013). https://money.cnn.com/2013/12/09/news/economy/america-economic-mobility/

wealthy to redistribute wealth to help the poor become more upwardly mobile, tends to have stagnant growth in upward mobility overall.

Furthermore, the lack of affordable health insurance makes it difficult for many people to break out of the cycle of poverty when an illness can so easily bankrupt a family or individual. It has become all too common to see yet another Go Fund Me campaign online for your friend's aunt asking for help to cover the costs related to her lymphoma treatments because her 'catastrophic' health insurance plan had an outrageously high deductible.

The point here is not to critically dwell on the negative or delve into politics on either side of the spectrum, but to illustrate some reasons why life is out of balance in America. We are always hearing about the most recent rag to riches IPO that is now a Netflix Original series or about the latest piece of must-have exercise equipment like a Peloton bike which sometimes becomes a great overpriced clothes hanger. What we don't hear about is how difficult it really is to make it as a small business in the U.S. A recent survey from the Federal Reserve Bank showed that three out of ten small businesses said they would not make it through the pandemic without additional federal help. That means nine million small businesses are at risk of closing their doors permanently in 2021, yet they are the fabric of our country. The outlook is even more grim for minority owned businesses with eight out of ten reporting they are in financial distress due to the pandemic.[3] In addition, nearly 53 percent of small businesses surveyed

---

[3] Brooks. (2021). https://www.cbsnews.com/news/small-business-federal-aid-pandemic/

do not expect to return to pre-Covid levels of operation for at least six months. It is hard enough running a small business in the best of times. The past two years have been anything but the best of times and is a testament to the precarious lifestyle faced by many.

We all know the divorce rate is high, too. In fact, America has one of the highest divorce rates in the world. Currently, the average divorce rate for people between 25-39 years of age is 24 out of 1,000 people and there are over 750,000 divorces in the U.S. every year. "Gray divorce" has risen dramatically over the past 30 years – divorces among those aged 50 and over has doubled over the past ten years.

Does it come as a surprise to learn that 70 percent of small businesses fail? Running and maintaining a successful small business is sometimes harder than being married! Then again, that really depends on who you choose to marry. We are fed a continual social media diet of how easy it looks to start your own business and make your first million. To illustrate this point, we now have countless incubators, accelerators, and grant programs across the U.S. to support startups – but they rarely offer a full suite of business tools to help sustain these businesses long-term which supports the failure statistic. I attended a free webinar recently as an audit exercise to prove my theory and as I suspected, the speaker did not disappoint. She sold her "millionaire" scam pitch with a smile and told the audience if we paid her today in full, that she could show us how to create a million-dollar business using her blueprint AND get a special bonus – just like an old-school used car salesman. "Paid in full! Paid in full! Paid in full and start today!" she yelled, like a bad 90's rap song you can't get out of your head.

The reality is much different. The reasons that most small businesses fail, according to Investopedia, is due to a lack of sufficient capital, poor management, inadequate business planning, and overblowing marketing budgets focused on tactics. In other words, cash flow problems, which is nothing new, are just a recurring theme now.

Now that I have your attention, I believe there is another important reason why several businesses fail often missing from the familiar laundry list of causes. Many people who start businesses chase money and profits before supporting their people and their purpose.

We are so consumed with catching that gold ring – the cash – that we miss a much more rewarding path to success that is both monetary and purpose-driven. There are exceptions: Take Because International, for example, is a company built around the ability to provide adjustable shoes (up to five sizes!) for the underserved populations who need them. An idea born from global travel, the founder returned home and decided he wanted to help make a difference in people's lives by offering a basic necessity – shoes. His mission and purpose were to develop a product that helps alleviate poverty and create positive impact. He then took those funds and developed an accelerator to support startups that build similar types of global products.

Then there is nendo, a Japanese company, that created a non-inflatable soccer ball which is assembled from 54 separate parts that the user can put together themselves before play, with the ability to personalize the ball as they assemble it. Inspired by the structure of traditional woven Japanese bamboo, the ball is created for easy repair, a feature that is especially useful for impoverished neighborhoods around the world.

What is concerning is a UK emerging sector called "Tech for Good" which includes companies who leverage technology for social impact, and yet they can't seem to get the funding they need to scale. According to Forbes, "investors and shareholders focus too much on short term financial gains, rather than long term sustainability," leaving the emerging sector unable to scale. It makes a plea for more "patient capital," having named those few VC funds that do invest in the sector.[4] What's wrong with this picture? It seems greed is currently still ahead of good.

When organizations choose a different path and keep an eye on shared purpose instead of just shareholder value, they end up creating energy, meaning, and fostering motivation and ownership in their ranks. I have seen countless bright sparks that were promising startups burn out after three years on the altar of a profits-first mentality.

By contrast, companies that are purpose-driven generate cultures of collaboration and ownership, thereby increasing employee satisfaction and buy-in. It is human nature to want to be part of something bigger than ourselves. Why else would sporting events, concerts, and religious conventions still appeal to so many people when the alternative could be sitting quietly at home on our couches swiping our smartphones? It's because humans long to belong on some level and we can catch a natural high from being part of something.

---

[4] Welsh. (2019). https://www.forbes.com/sites/johnwelsheurope/2019/04/24/20-tech-for-social-good-startups-to-watch-as-tech-nation-tackles-signs-of-the-sector-stalling/?sh=1892093b300b

When you communicate your organization's purpose, your "why" (thanks Simon Sinek!), you help people feel a sense of ownership of that purpose. Companies like Ritz Carlton, famous for their customer service, do this well. In a recent interview with Forbes Magazine, the general manager of the Ritz Carlton in San Francisco, Yael Ron, said, "To create an exceptional customer experience, you don't start with the customer; you start with the employee. This surprises a lot of people, and a lot of people get this wrong." The employees at Ritz Carlton, known as 'Ladies and Gentlemen' are considered the gemstones of the organization and are embraced, supported, empowered, and given a degree of autonomy to make customer service decisions without seeking permission from upper management.[5] This is a practice still rare in most organizations today.

While we have discussed the statistics of how hard it is to succeed as a small business or startup in America, the fact is that some do succeed. Companies like DoorDash and AirBnB ranked Number Two and Number One, respectively, on the short list of biggest IPOs of 2020 and during a pandemic, no less.[6] What are the characteristics that help people succeed? There are several and we will delve into all of them in the chapters to come. Two of the primary reasons, which have been targets of ample research over the past few years, are grit and failure.

---

[5] Solomon. (2020). www.forbes.com/sites/micahsolomon/2020/02/23/how-to-bring-ritz-carlton-caliber-customer-service-to-any-type-of-business/?sh=74d545c7657d

[6] Haqqi. (2020). www.insidermonkey.com/blog/5-biggest-ipos-of-2020-916171/5/

According to Angela Duckworth, author of the bestselling *Grit: The Power of Passion and Perseverance*, her research has proven that it is not only talent or genius that is required for success, but long-term tenacity or what she terms *grit*, a combination of passion and perseverance. The even better news is that grit can be learned, it is not something that only lucky people are born with - and I am a big fan of learning new things.

The truth is, it is difficult to carve out the time to just sit back and achieve balance by quieting our minds, or by learning to cultivate a new trait like grit. In our constant, immediate *let's roll!* culture, jumping from one thing to the next without so much as a bathroom break or time for lunch, it can be hard to create space for this, much less read a book or do any kind of deep thinking. In Cal Newport's book *Deep Work*, he helps readers rediscover the human ability to think and focus deeply which requires setting aside scheduled time to do, a skill seriously under threat in our digital, always-on world.

"I insist on a lot of time being spent, almost every day, to just sit and think. That is very uncommon in American business...So I do more reading and thinking and make fewer impulse decisions than most people in business."

~ Warren Buffet

With constant competing priorities, it's important to make time to create better connected balance by looking at your life, your family, your business, or your work on a regular basis, especially if you are a startup. There are always 50,000 things on your to-do list, most of which can wait. The deep-thinking time won't happen unless you schedule it just like you schedule your workout. I want you to try it with me now. After reading this chapter, put this book down, turn off all your devices and let your mind wander quietly for 15 minutes. Go for a walk if that helps. Personally, I'm what they call a moving meditator, meaning I do my best thinking when I am in motion whether it's walking, running, swimming, hiking, or riding my bike. Take some focused time for yourself, preferably outside (maybe while you walk your dog!) and think about what is most important to you and then come back and jot down your thoughts. This will give you a chance to get off your hamster wheel even for a little while so you can breathe. This is the first step to finding better balance as you begin to move away from incoherence and towards more personal alignment. That wheel will be there waiting for you when you get back, it always is.

How do we move from incoherence into better alignment? A life lived out of balance yet in line with the unquestioned dogmas of corporate culture that predominates our landscape, starts with exploring what that life of balance might look like, a balance between work, personal life, health, and spirit. Chapter Two, Balance, will look at balancing masculine and feminine energy and the heart-brain coherence connection. When you are in the flow of coherence, you make better decisions in your business and for your life. Business has been missing its heart for a long time and now heart finally has a seat at the table in our emerging post-pandemic world.

Chapter Three is all about Connection. I will discuss the idea of trust and provide a core values exercise to help you identify yours if needed for better personal clarity. We will look at how being present in your business or your life allows you to see what wants to happen versus what *you* want to happen. I will discuss the concept of transformational presence, forcing agendas, and scheduling time just to think and be. We will explore how to find your own truth and ground yourself in it. I will then lead you on a brief trip through the history of education and the evolution of society over the past century to illustrate how we have outgrown many of the dogmatic beliefs of our culture. I believe one of the most important things you need to thrive in today's world is a growth mindset. This chapter will encourage you to examine whether your belief system is yours or something inherited from your family or society.

In Chapter Four, Trust, I will talk about how we are starved for human connection, especially now. I will examine Eastern cultural ideas of balance like Yin and Yang, innovative ideas about energy, Western ideology versus Eastern ideology versus the way we actually live our lives which is more dictated by our to-do list than anything else. I will ask the question: What if we adopted a focus on the energy of being rather than doing? What if we were less focused on separateness and individuality? What would our experiences be if we were more focused on community and an integrated approach to life and work? Through stories and examples, I will illustrate how to embrace conscious decision-making with clear intent to notice all the warning red flags waving at you when they crop up, not later.

Chapter Five is an exploration of Failure and how to embrace it as our best teacher. One of my favorite sayings is: "I eat failure for breakfast, so I can dine on success for dinner." We will look at how the characteristics of tenacity and grit are sometimes more important to future success than talent or brains.

In Chapter Six, Karma, I will delve into the idea of how the energy you put out into the world comes right back to you as we examine the use of energy principles to explore different ways of thinking and being. I will share ways to apply quantum physics to a world that still clings to a mechanistic model of the Universe, despite science supporting all evidence to the contrary.

Finally, in Chapter Seven, Flow, I will offer a series of takeaways on how to live a life that flows, rather than bumps and grinds and twerks since I have no interest in competing with Miley Cyrus in that area. You will learn how to identify your unique value, keep your sense of humor intact (most of the time!), and strive to take on new challenges outside of your comfort zone. You really can do whatever you want if you step away from your limiting beliefs and become open to possibility.

As you read this book, find time to think about the chapter takeaways and identify the things you feel you are subconsciously forcing to happen at work and in life, instead of focusing on the things that happen easily, or *want to happen* which are more aligned with your intent. I'll get into this idea of transformational presence more later, but for now, go do it.

You'll be surprised by what surfaces when you make the time to think, I promise. Now off you go!

KEY TAKEAWAYS

- Schedule 15 minutes a day just to think by yourself. That's it. Nothing else. If you can get outside to do it, even better.

- Discover your "why" by doing some real soul searching, so you can understand what makes you tick. For help getting started, pick up a copy of Simon Sinek's book *Start with Why*; his podcasts can also be found at www. simonsinek.com

- Identify 1-3 areas in your life you know are incoherent and out of alignment with who you really are and what you want. Focus on how you can shift those areas to a place that feels better.

- Take a personal inventory of your task list and remove a few things from your plate. Learn how to slow down, relax, and take a nap if you don't know how to already. There is great benefit to stillness.

- Make a conscious decision to get more sleep and exercise regularly. The body repairs itself during deep sleep and exercise improves sleep quality, plus helps you fall asleep more quickly. Winner!

Chapter Two

Balance

"Life is like riding a bicycle. To keep your balance, you must keep moving."

~ Albert Einstein

Simone Biles, the champion U.S. gymnast, garnered international attention when she withdrew from competition during the Japan Summer Olympics in 2021 due to a case of the "twisties." A well-known and feared syndrome among gymnasts that manifests differently across athletes and other sports, it is a condition where the mind disconnects from the body, leaving the gymnast unable to know where she is in mid-air and whether she is going to be able to land safely or not. Fortunately for Biles, she decided to put her health and safety before her desire to win at all costs and withdrew before she injured herself. Smart.

Biles received criticism from some camps for being a "quitter" and no doubt not towing the typical agenda of pushing through the pain, whether mental or physical. She was overwhelmingly supported by other athletes who recognized her decision as actually being the most courageous one since the stakes were at an all-time high. For an airborne gymnast, experiencing a disconnect between mind and body is different from a missed basket or shot, it is the very real possibility of never being able to walk again if something goes wrong during a competition.

There have been numerous other cases where the athlete was not so lucky and ended up being either gravely injured or paralyzed for life. Jacoby Miles, 23, was paralyzed from the chest down after landing on her neck during a gymnastics routine during a similar bout of the twisties. Melanie Coleman, a gymnast from Southern Connecticut State, was killed in 2019 when she fell off the uneven bars.[7] No one is immune

---

[7] Apstein. (2021). https://www.si.com/olympics/2021/08/02/simone-biles-twisties-physical-risk-former-gymnasts-left-paralyzed

to the effects of disconnection and it's not just gymnasts. In golf, the twisties are known as the yips. A few of the pro golfers who have experienced this affliction are Ernie Els, David Duval, Pádraig Harrington, Bernhard Langer, and Ben Hogan.[8]

The Twisties are a perfect, but extreme, example of what happens to us when our body and our mind is out of sync. In this chapter we will explore the idea around how much better we are able to function, both personally and professionally, when we strive for balance in our lives.

I have had a few bad bike accidents. As I mentioned, I'm a moving meditator and love to be outside as there is nothing like feeling my body sailing through space and time like a kid racing her big wheel down a hill. I can easily unplug from life's daily grind while cruising down the trail on my bike – a favorite escape. All it takes is a slight distraction often caused by my sudden lack of ability to stay present in the moment, and the next thing I know I've rolled over something on the ground and I'm flying over my handlebars. It's like an out of body experience watching myself from above as I bounce down the bike trail in slow motion. Luckily, I have cat-like reflexes and can stop, drop, and roll on a dime, so most of the time, I don't get seriously hurt. I've learned to stay dialed in and focused for my own safety.

These are dangerous examples of balance gone wrong. However, balance can mean allowing what wants to happen in your business as opposed to what *you* want to happen. It can move you from a place of forcing agendas to allowing a flow of what needs to happen instead. I experienced this with my consulting work while discussing new potential partnerships

---

[8] *Yips.* (2021). https://en.wikipedia.org/wiki/Yips

with other business owners. It seemed like our companies were a great fit – a meeting of minds and agendas, similar proclivities, and similar personalities. I was excited about the possibility of collaborating after successfully navigating the preliminary stages of a new business relationship through a series of Zoom meetings, as one does these days.

I suggested we formalize our partnership and started to get prescriptive about how we might proceed. I suddenly had to ask myself, am I trying to push this? To force a certain path when we might not really be aligned? We decided to go back to our corners and do the respective research around the points we had discussed, then get back together and share all our findings. A week later, excited and ready to roll, I reached back out and said, "Here's what I think we should do; here's how we can package our services together; and I've proactively looked at some legal agreements." I noticed an energy shift almost immediately. Everything cooled off and I didn't hear back for a couple of weeks. My initial impulse was to keep hammering it, to follow up right away. I had to sit back and ask myself again: am I forcing my agenda here? I realized I was operating from my old paradigm of taking the lead, pushing to get things done, and kicking ass and taking names rather than allowing what needed to happen, happen on its own time. Turns out the delay was all about timing as I seem to move faster than most when it comes to getting things done. There was interest but I was three steps ahead, ready to move, and once our timing was aligned, we would collaborate as the pandemic continues to impact business execution in many ways.

I have seen this scenario several times across various situations and have learned that, while it's productive, push energy doesn't always make for the best results. When overly focused on an outcome, you can miss the nuances along the way that are trying to tell and show you things both good and bad about what you are trying to do. When you slow down and pay attention to what wants to happen, it is amazing what shows up - and it's often better than you expect. I am still working on learning about how patience is a virtue. Damn.

TRANSFORMATIONAL PRESENCE

When you start to focus on what is happening around you and you're present in the moment, you can engage transformational presence principles to infer what wants to happen, versus what you're forcing to happen. This is a fundamental piece of awareness necessary because too many of us are operating on autopilot with what we think we should be doing stemming from old belief patterns or from things we are told we should be doing or should be concerned with. Or worse, that awareness seems to take a backseat when we realize that money, profit, or revenue targets are the prime motivator behind our actions.

Transformational Presence is a theory of leadership where leaders collaborate with their teams beyond their immediate self-interests to drive change. The concept of transformational leadership was initially developed by James V. Downton and presidential biographer, James MacGregor Burns. The idea is that leaders and their teams help each other advance to higher and higher levels of "morality and motivation."[9]

---

[9] Bass. (1999). *Two Decades of Research and Development In Transformational Leadership.*

Through the strength of their vision and personality, transformational leaders can inspire followers to change expectations, perceptions, and motivations to work towards common goals. Martin Luther King is widely recognized as being a transformational leader in the way in which he led, exhorting people to live by their highest ideals and encouraging his followers with the implicit message that he expected the best out of them, and they could deliver it.

Like we discussed in the last chapter with the Ritz Carlton example of their exemplary customer service, I can only surmise that the CEO of that company must exhibit transformational leadership qualities as they encourage their 'Ladies and Gentlemen' to have autonomy over specific jobs and are empowered to make decisions on their own.

It is not just Martin Luther King or CEOs of global corporations that can exhibit transformational presence and, in turn, transformational leadership. There have been leaders throughout the ages who were said to have inspired their followers in similar ways. Take for example, Mahatma Gandhi, the revered nonviolent resister who led the successful campaign for India's independence from British rule in the 1930s. He championed peaceful protests and campaigned for the rights of India's poor, garnering folk hero status at home in India and throughout the world. Meanwhile, he vexed England's Prime Minister at the time, Winston Churchill, who called him "...a fakir of a type well known in the East, striding half-naked up the steps of the Vice-regal palace....to parley on equal terms with the representative of the King-Emperor."[10]

---

[10] Herman. (2008). *Gandhi & Churchill: The Epic Rivalry that Destroyed an Empire and Forged Our Age.*

Gandhi's transformational leadership was so successful he threatened the entire British empire and Churchill was afraid that, "British themselves would give up out of pacifism and misplaced conscience."[11]

Rest assured, we do not need to wear loincloths or dedicate ourselves to regular fasting (or juicing for that matter!) to embrace the ideals of transformational leadership. The four distinct behaviors associated with these kinds of leaders are known as the "Four I's" – inspirational motivation, idealized influence, intellectual stimulation, and individualized consideration. Inspirational motivation translates as being able to inspire people to be interested in a project, encouraging people to own their work, understanding your teams' strengths and weaknesses, being adaptable, setting high, yet reasonable goals, and creating a shared vision for an organization.

Idealized influence is when you lead by example, are committed, and fully ethical in your dealings with your team. This inspires your team to follow you. Intellectual stimulation is when you encourage your team to think for themselves, are open to new ideas from them, and embrace failure as a chance for learning. Finally, individualized consideration is when leaders can exhibit and communicate genuine concern for their employees and team members, helping them to self-actualize and grow in their roles wherever possible.

What does transformational leadership or presence have to do with balance? Primarily, if you are acting from a place of chaos and constant drama and disruption, you cannot be effective in any of the above-mentioned realms as a leader. It takes a balanced approach to people and projects to be able

---

[11] Ibid.

to lead effectively. It is tempting to turn to nature for proof of the need for balance, as there has long been a 'balance of nature' theory. It would be too convenient for my argument if I could point a finger at a nearby elm tree and say, "There, look at that very balanced tree! That's how we should be, see?" In reality, nature is stormy, dynamic, and chaotic. In fact, the Balance of Nature has been largely discredited by ecologists since the second half of the 20th century and replaced instead by Chaos Theory and Catastrophe Theory.

Chaos Theory is an interdisciplinary theory which proposes that within the seeming randomness of chaotic complex systems, there are underlying patterns, interconnectedness, constant feedback loops, repetition, self-similarity, fractals, and an inherent, underlying self-organization. It's just like when you take on one more thing when your plate is already full, but for some reason you decide you can do it all and will prove that to your ego or die trying. It is sort of like going to college while playing a sport, holding down a part-time job, and expecting to be able to breathe while having a social life. My college experience was nothing short of the underpinnings of Chaos Theory which taught me early how to become a professional multitasker. It wasn't until later in life I decided to retire that title as doing "everything" all the time doesn't scale, is exhausting, and it certainly doesn't provide much room for anything fun.

BIOMIMICRY

Maybe we can't say nature is totally balanced, but we can certainly find answers and innovative solutions to humanity's problems in nature's systems. This is called biomimicry which is, technically speaking, the simulation of the models, systems, and aspects of nature for the purpose of solving complex human problems. Biomimicry is being applied across many disciplines such as finding ways to make wings more aerodynamic or colors more vivid. It gave the world Velcro, created by the Swiss engineer Georges de Mestral after he noticed how burrs stuck to his clothes. Mercedes and Opel cars have implemented design software that mimics the ways trees and bones disseminate strength and loads. The whirling patterns of kelp, nautilus, and whelks were the inspiration for a fan created by Pax Scientific and a greenhouse irrigated by saltwater in the Qatari desert uses condensation and evaporation elements inspired by a camel's nose.[12]

YIN AND YANG

While biomimicry looks to forms in nature to bring balance and innovation into human creations, the Far East has been integrating ideas of balance into their culture for centuries. Yin and Yang represent an ancient Chinese philosophy of dualism. The idea is that opposite, or contrarian, forces are interdependent in the natural world and represent a prism through which we can guide our own actions. In Chinese cosmology, the universe is created out of a chaos of matter which is then organized into cycles of Yin and Yang, rendering objects and lives as one or the other.

---

[12] Vanderbilt. (2012). https://www.smithsonianmag.com/science-nature/how-biomimicry-is-inspiring-human-innovation-17924040/

Yin is seen as the receptive principle, Yang as the active principle, and each has historically been categorized as feminine and masculine principles. However, other dualities that Yin and Yang are reflected in are light and dark, expanding and contracting, fire and water. The image of Yin and Yang represent interconnected but opposing forces. Yet there is an inherent balance in the image. So, how does this concept apply when you are trying to find more balance or be strategic in your business or life?

Often, the competitive demand between your company's internal needs (enterprise versus employees) and external needs (shareholders/investors versus customers/community) is a typical challenge. Discussions about solutions and plans are usually based on the application of resources to one plan or another. We tend to think of requirements as separate and distinct, but in fact they often are closely interrelated. If the needs of the people on your team are not considered, there will not be enough resources to meet the needs of stakeholders. The two are interdependent, and the needs of both must be constantly balanced and managed. Yin and Yang are not mutually exclusive -- they are interdependent. The solution to this dilemma is to include both solutions. Obvious, right? Guess again.

We live in a black and white culture that is dominated by the idea of *either/or* not *yes/and*, along with less acceptance to tolerating dichotomies or two contradictory ideas at the same time. Authors Jim Collins and Jerry Porras explore this idea in their book *Built to Last: Successful Habits of Visionary Companies*. They introduce the idea of the "Genius of the And" which, ironically, is the foundation of improvisation comedy.

Using the concept of *yes/and*, one improviser starts a scene, and makes 'an offer.' The other improvisor in the scene must accept that offer by, in effect, saying, "Yes, and," adding to the premise, the story, or the sketch. Then a scene can go somewhere. Dualities exist. They are part of nature and a part of us.

Since I love to laugh, appreciate quick wit, and have been watching several types of comedy for decades, I thought it would be fun to learn the nuts and bolts of writing standup, comedic timing, and the art of delivery to see how that could potentially be applied to business presentations. Most people enjoy a good laugh which also feels good, so why not make work more fun? Through a personal connection, I was introduced to a professional British comedian who was teaching online while the London clubs were closed during the pandemic. I was sure I could learn a few things from him. After four Zoom sessions and a lot of laughs, I had a full understanding of how to write a bit, the significant differences between standup, improv, and the need for *yes/and* which I could now effectively apply to any situation. Maybe I'll even find an open mic night to test my new knowledge.

The word paradox means *the existence of two opposing ideas at the same time.* Within a paradox is both a problem and a tension to release that problem. Instead of our usual knee jerk reaction to view this in a negative light, perhaps we could reframe our view that this interdependence of the dilemma and resolving tension is instead healthy and, if we allow it, may yield new insights or solutions. An easier way to put it: How many shades of grey can be tolerated in each situation? Definitely more than fifty, but who's counting? Not every solution or answer is black and white – quite literally.

These are some areas where this kind of paradoxical thinking might prove beneficial:

- Working in the enterprise or on it
- Short term vision or results versus long term growth and results
- Stability versus innovation
- The needs of the individual versus the needs of the team
- Leading strongly while simultaneously encouraging autonomy and motivation from within

There are, without a doubt, times in my life when I have been off kilter. I have had to consciously learn to modify some of these behaviors that contributed to my lack of balance. I found that, over the years, too much drive energy isn't helpful with the alignment of my masculine (left brain) and feminine (right brain) when those energies were off. Like when your left brain is relentlessly leading a charge to reach a goal with no time or room for the creative right side to kick in and help keep things balanced. This mindset creates misalignment, stress, and if left unchecked, eventually illness. I learned through exploring the alternative healing practice of Reiki that you absolutely can balance these energies across your body, which might sound too woo-woo for some, but I am a "try anything once" type of curious learner who is always looking for ways to improve. Each time I have a Reiki session, it enables me to create the energetic shifts I need, when I need them to achieve better connected balance. From this practice, I have been able to learn how to slow down and intuitively 'sense' and feel the best course of action in a situation, not push a preconceived idea of what I think should be happening.

I find joy in helping others succeed but not in controlling their journey based on any preconceived notions I may have or think I have. As I mentor students and startup companies, I no longer provide immediate advice to the problems I see. I start with a series of questions to ensure I understand the full picture, then help them potentially arrive at the solutions they may infer by themselves, which is much more fun and empowering for them versus being told. Listening to their perspective, learning what they are trying to do, and helping them discover how they feel about what is happening currently is more productive than providing a quick hit solution to a perceived problem and robbing them of the opportunity to learn. Plus, this approach also creates a better relationship of trust and understanding when both perspectives can work together toward a shared goal. While that may seem pretty obvious, society and the business landscape has taught us to quickly problem solve on the fly at all costs and rewards such behavior. This approach actually cuts off the energy of a situation, damages relationships, and doesn't allow the space or time for things to evolve as they want to or should.

If you have ever read a book on dating in your life, then you will be familiar with the idea of "putting on your dress" as a woman making sure that you are highlighting your best feminine side. This is a tired suggestion for most of us, but nevertheless we have been programmed and wired to hear these 'truisms' as the way a woman can try to get ahead in a man's world. This has certainly been true in such male-dominated fields as technology where I spent most of my career.

The truth is, we as women don't need to put on our dresses and men don't need to stick a pickaxe in their belt loop, for that matter. Forget all these bad, old-school stereotypes: what we all need is better balance. Developing a combination of both masculine and feminine energy is a more effective path for success in business and in life. I think the ancient Chinese philosophers would agree.

HEARTMATH

In the past 40 years, the effect of heart activity on brain function has been extensively studied. These studies focused on the effect of heart activity that occurs during a short period of time on several consecutive maximum heartbeats. Scientists at the HeartMath Institute[13] have expanded this scientific research body by studying how large-scale heart activity patterns affect brain function.

Their research has shown that different heart patterns have varying rhythms of heart activity (accompanied by different emotional states) and have different effects on cognitive and emotional functions. It has also shown that the heart's electromagnetic field is five thousand times greater than the electromagnetic field of the brain. So, logically solving problems only using your brain means you are missing out on that extra energy boost. During periods of stress or negative emotions, when the heart rhythm pattern is unstable and disorderly like a drunk zigzagging around the bar just before closing time, the corresponding neural signal patterns from

---

[13] https://www.heartmath.com

the heart to the brain can inhibit higher cognitive functions. This limits our ability to think clearly, remember, learn, reason, and make effective decisions. Now you can understand why, when we are stressed out, we often act impulsively and recklessly. During periods of stress or negative emotions, information from the heart to the brain can have a profound effect on the emotional processes of the brain, creating heightened emotional impact.

Conversely, in a positive emotional state, a more orderly and stable input pattern from the heart to the brain will have the opposite effect: it promotes cognitive function, strengthens positive emotions and emotional stability, and is called coherence. This means that learning to improve heart rate consistency by encouraging and accessing our positive emotions is beneficial for the entire body, and profoundly affects our perception, thinking, feeling, and performance.

Although the heart is undoubtedly an extraordinary pump, what I find fascinating is that over the last three centuries or so of human civilization, the function of the heart has been defined as a machine that pumps blood (in Western scientific thinking). Historically, in almost all cultures across the world, the heart has played a more diverse role in the human system and is considered the source of wisdom, spiritual perception, thought, and emotion. More recent scientific research has begun to provide evidence that many of these long-standing associations may not be merely spiritual concepts or metaphors. These developments have prompted scientists to review and expand their understanding of the role of this magical organ again and without a monkey in a tiny coat and hat.

In the new field of neurocardiology, scientists discovered that the heart has its own inner nervous system, a complex neural network that deserves to be called the "heart-brain." This Brain 2.0 has more than 40,000 neurons, allowing the heart to independently detect and process information, make decisions, and even demonstrate a learning and memory ability. Suddenly, the heart seems like the smartest kid in the class, always too shy to raise her hand. Studies have also shown that the heart is a hormonal gland that produces and secretes many hormones and neurotransmitters that have a profound effect on brain and body functions. Oxytocin, the "love hormone" or "bonding hormone," is among the hormones produced by the heart - not the brain. Science has only just begun to understand the effects of the electromagnetic field created by the heart in humans and in animals, horses specifically, but there is evidence that the information contained in the heart's strong field plays a critical role in timing in the human body and can affect other people around us, too.

All these things, whether it is HeartMath, Transformational Presence, or Yin and Yang, are tools to help you achieve coherence within yourself and how you show up in the world. The more we can connect to our intuition, despite always being taught in business and society in general not *to feel or not to lead with emotion*, the better. That thinking is part of the school of thought that is more masculine-oriented and suggests that leading with emotions is wrong – it's too feminine. What is needed is a view that is better balanced. HeartMath offers us that construct and various tools, because when our brains and hearts are balanced and connected, we are more productive, we don't make hasty decisions, we think about the big picture.

> "Balance is not something you find,
> it's something you create."
>
> ~ Jana Kingsford

I can imagine that Henry David Thoreau had some good HeartMath going on. Thoreau was an early American naturist, poet, essayist, and philosopher, most known for his writings and quarantining himself – without an actual pandemic – in the woods at Walden Pond to write and be in nature. Thoreau took part in what we, in our 21st century workaholic culture, would call some serious deep thinking. For us to do deep thinking, we have to schedule it in our calendars, wedged between our meetings, workouts, errands, personal needs, and appointments. The point of this is not to wax prolific on how life was so much better a century and a half ago, but to remind us that our human urges to engage in thought, solitude, time in nature, and creative acts, are integral to our health and our ability to thrive. Without these things, we become unbalanced, frenetic, splintered, stressed, and stretched until we end up making ourselves sick, mentally, and sometimes physically.

We do not need to alter our lives so drastically as Thoreau did to find balance. Nevertheless, let's pause and appreciate his words:

I went to the woods because I wished to live deliberately, to front only the essential facts of life, and see if I could not learn what it had to teach, and not, when I came to die, discover that I had not lived. I did not wish to live what was not life, living is so dear; nor did I wish to practice resignation, unless it was quite necessary. I wanted to live deep and suck out all the marrow of life, to live so sturdily and Spartan-like as to put to rout all that was not life, to cut a broad swath and shave close, to drive life into a corner, and reduce it to its lowest terms, and, if it proved to be mean, why then to get the whole and genuine meanness of it, and publish its meanness to the world; or if it were sublime, to know it by experience, and be able to give a true account of it in my next excursion.[14]

KEY TAKEAWAYS

∽ When you are feeling disconnected in your life, take time to reflect on where you might be out of balance to avoid your own version of the twisties. Take time out in nature to make your own mini-Thoreau-like retreat.

∽ Become a transformational leader and inspire others to change expectations, perceptions, and motivations to work towards common goals as a team.

∽ Embrace your Yin and Yang and appreciate both masculine and feminine qualities as we need a balance of both in each of us.

∽ Look for patterns and inspiration in nature to draw analogies, create meaning or innovations in your own life like Biomimicry does.

∽ Learn more about HeartMath tools to create coherence as the heart is as much a center of intelligence as the brain is, so give it due respect. www.heartmath.org

---

[14] Thoreau. (2017). *Walden: Life in the Woods.*

Chapter Three

Connection

"He that falls in love with himself
will have no rivals."

~ Benjamin Franklin

One of the most fundamental human needs involves the power of touch. We may communicate through words, but we are sensory creatures and need to connect to one another through touch. Studies have shown that the more routine affection that partners experience, the more they feel satisfied by their partner's touch. For both men and women, lower levels of routine affection led to relationship dissatisfaction. It is not only couples that need touch, as we know intuitively. Studies have been done for years in neonatal units with premature babies as volunteer "snugglers" spend time cuddling babies to boost their well-being. A former colleague of mine who volunteers for this role at a local hospital and can confirm the positive effects. Nurses and doctors report that the cuddles have an immediate and measurable impact on the infants. "Their blood oxygenation starts to climb, meaning the baby is relaxed and is breathing deeper. The doctors say cuddling leads to better tolerance of pain, more stable body temperature and even stronger vital signs."[15]

Not just babies need cuddles. Over the past few years, enterprising 'cuddlers' have set up actual brick and mortar cuddle shops around the world. Samantha Hess runs Cuddle Up to Me in Portland, Oregon where her team has been offering cuddles in one of four themed rooms since 2013. Yes, this is a real thing, and she is not the only one. Apparently, there is a booming business for platonic cuddles. And no, you can't upgrade for additional services and all clothes stay on as this is not a *massage* parlor. Hess says, "It's about making people

---

[15] Wright and Netter. (2014). https://abcnews.go.com/blogs/headlines/2014/03/cuddling-babies-hospital-volunteers-show-the-power-of-human-touch

feel worthy for who they are today. ... I love knowing that people know that they are accepted, and they aren't going to be alone anymore."[16]

Hess reports a wide range of clientele, from divorcees to amputees, and sessions can last from 15 minutes to up to an hour. Some of her clients are military vets who come home from serving tours abroad and experience a personal and emotional disconnect. This disconnect was necessary so they could fight and complete their tours of duty. Once home, that disconnect interferes with their trying to integrate back into their lives post-tour and many experience PTSD. In 2008, Hollywood decided to make a movie titled *The Hurt Locker* highlighting this painful PTSD related disconnection. The film starred Jeremy Renner as Staff Sergeant William James and he was nominated for an Academy Award for his amazing performance. In recent years, the drug MDMA has been used to help heal post-traumatic stress disorder; non-pharmaceutical therapies include therapy dogs and horses.[17] Should it come as any surprise that professional snugglers can do some of this therapy work, too?

Hess's employees undergo a 40-hour training program on platonic cuddling to meet the needs of their wide-ranging clients hungry for touch. What I find fascinating is that on the other side of the pond this phenomenon is also evolving. A German business called cuddlers.net is offering similar services to Hess. They, too, are focused on the importance of human

---

[16] Murray. (2014). https://abcnews.go.com/US/professional-cuddler/story?id=26973763

[17] Mitchell, et al. (2021). https://www.nature.com/articles/s41591-021-01336-3

touch as a basic need outside of sex and are even hosting cuddle parties! While this might all seem a bit 'touchy-feely,' it goes to the heart of what this chapter is about. Humans need connection. We are especially starved for connection after months of enduring a worldwide pandemic in which many of us were quarantined in our homes with only our screens for company. I would suggest, better to have screens than have nothing. However, even that does not replace the need for physical, in person contact as connections can be powerful and sometimes life changing, given the chance.

The truth is, we are all taught by society to look outside ourselves to find the right connections we need to make us whole, be it the perfect job, the house, a car, a relationship, a lifestyle, or a soul mate. Society feeds us the separate story from birth, which tells us we are not whole unless we are constantly seeking contentment outside of ourselves.

Whatever that deal of the day is, whether it is the white house with the picket fence with two kids and a dog or the Peloton that is going to make our butt and core fabulous, it's really just marketing to feed our capitalistic society. What we really need to do is go inside and connect to ourselves for our energy source and find our center to ground in our truth. Yes, outside connection helps support our emotional needs, but it is the inside connection to self-love that is the core foundation of what will make us truly happy.

I can remember working on various projects throughout my career that included some key people I met and had great connections with. These connections influenced me depending on what was going on at that time in my life and were the types of relationships that made work fun. They were supportive and provided insight even if we all were not on the same page in terms of perspective. Looking back now, it's that feeling of connection and being productive that helps us feel good. It is why women lunch with their girlfriends or men grab beers to watch the game, or people go on dates as everyone connects in different ways. It is why some people attend church or go to sporting events and concerts. It is as if a shared connection is the ultimate prize, and how we choose to find it, to each her own. Society continues, however, to teach us to look outside ourselves to material objects, money, or work to feel good or for our happiness. This becomes a slippery slope of unmet expectations and disappointment especially since happiness is an inside job. Just ask a recent retiree how hard it is to transition out of the workforce when personal happiness is tied to a career.

A recent episode of the podcast *This American Life* tracked young people and "hook up" culture in post-pandemic America, offering some surprising findings. Millennials and Gen-Zers are hooking up and choosing casual sex far less often than one would think, especially after months of lockdowns. The data revealed that, more often than not, young people reported going home with partners and are cuddling rather than having sex. What is going on here? Again, I suspect it is our fundamental need for connection with others that is getting lost in our always-on, 24/7 screen culture.[18]

In our current landscape where work from home has become the norm more than the exception, it is more critical

---

[18] *Episode 697: Alone Together*, transcript. (2020). https://www.thisamericanlife.org/697/transcript

than ever that we find creative ways to connect with others. Without connection, we have limited balance. As you may have begun to suspect, I am putting together a recipe book of sorts on the elements needed for us to thrive and evolve. Buffer's 2019 State of Remote Work survey found that loneliness was the second biggest struggle for remote workers, after 'unplugging from work.'[19] Experts have even suggested that chronic loneliness is as bad for your health as smoking 15 cigarettes a day. Even worse, a Cigna survey found that people who reported not having a good work-life balance to be seven points lonelier than their peers. The loneliness scale in America went from 54 percent in 2018 to 61 percent in 2019 with most people reporting the reasons being not enough social support, too few meaningful social interactions, poor physical and mental health, and finally, not enough balance in their lives.[20]

There is little debate that on some level we all need and want some level of connection to each other whether platonically, romantically, or professionally, which is necessary and healthy. There are other forms of connection, too. One of those forms is being connected to our bodies and listening to the cues it sends for what it wants and needs. And no, I don't mean yet another Krispy Kreme doughnut. Although, raspberry filled Krispy Kremes are my kryptonite. While I do try to make healthy food choices, I would be lying if I didn't

---

[19] *State of Remote Work.* (n.d.). https://buffer.com/state-of-remote -work-2019

[20] *Loneliness and the Workplace.* (2020). https://www.cigna.com/ static/www-cigna-com/docs/about-us/newsroom/studies-and-reports/ combatting-loneliness/cigna-2020-loneliness-infographic.pdf

admit that doughnuts have motivated more than a few runs in my time. When I was in high school, one of my teammates and I used to run across the street to Dunkin Donuts to split a dozen before our home track meets, so we could run like the wind on all that sugar. Yep, that's six each.

I have a good friend, Anna (not the same friend from my doughnut runs), who is a fitness trainer and a rowing coach focused on strength, mobility, and performance for the past 30 plus years. She also works with various levels of athletes one-on-one from Olympic level to weekend warrior helping them learn how to become more consciously aware in their sport, so they can achieve their highest levels of potential and their best outcomes. Her conscious connection work is built into every training plan to ensure an athlete is firing on all cylinders across mind, body, and spirit for complete alignment and optimal performance. As we discussed with the Simone Biles story, athletes are the perfect example of the importance of connection and alignment to our bodies. It is not only athletes, however, who need to be acutely aware of this connection.

I suggest that the more we are connected to the wisdom within our bodies by drawing on tools like HeartMath and listening to our intuition, the more we can begin to operate from a connected energy of being rather than doing. While I believe having a growth mindset is a powerful ingredient to becoming the best version of yourself, the constant need for change and improvement leads to a malady of constant doing rather than trying to simply exist in the present. Eckhart Tolle wrote extensively about his discovery that being in the eternal present gave him more joy than anything else.

After struggling with long periods of depression, one night in 1977 at the age of 29, he experienced an "inner transformation":

I couldn't live with myself any longer. And in this a question arose without an answer: who is the 'I' that cannot live with the self? What is the self? I felt drawn into a void! I didn't know at the time that what really happened was the mind-made self, with its heaviness, its problems, that lives between the unsatisfying past and the fearful future, collapsed. It dissolved. The next morning, I woke up and everything was so peaceful. The peace was there because there was no self. Just a sense of presence or "beingness," just observing and watching.[21]

Tolle began to feel a potential sense of calm. He suspended studying for a Ph.D. for about two years, spending most of his time sitting on a park bench in Russell Square in Central London, "in a state of deep happiness," and, "watching the world pass by." He spent some time sleeping on friends' couches, took refuge with monks in a Buddhist monastery, and slept rough on Hampstead Heath, a huge park in North London. His family thought he had lost his mind. Who would have predicted he would go on to become a bestselling author and icon for generations of spiritual seekers?

Rest assured; you do not have to go through extremes like Eckhart to start experiencing more being in your life rather than mindlessly going through the motions in a constant state of doing. As we discussed in the last chapter, we all have

---

[21] Scobie. (2003). https://clairescobie.com/wp-content/uploads/2014/12/On-Guru-Eckhart-Tolle_Aug03.pdf

both masculine and feminine energies and one more reason to live a more balanced life is to keep these energies within us balanced. Again, we can look to Chinese culture and their philosophy of Yin and Yang for inspiration. When one of these energies becomes dominant, we can experience burn out, fatigue, and general feelings of disconnection.

Feminine energies are typically associated with things like intuition, creativity, compassion, and understanding while masculine energies are associated with action, logic, adventure, loyalty, confidence, focus, and efficiency. Our culture does encourage a masculine, ego-driven way of behaving, while traits such as empathy, nurturing, or intuition tend to be undervalued and discouraged in the workplace. I believe there is a place for all these traits within each of us and in each arena we find ourselves in. The more we embrace and allow these traits to be expressed in ourselves and in others, the more balanced we will feel.

While it is important to find what works for you to give you a sense of grounding and connectivity, I can personally recommend the healing properties of water. After all, I like to think it is no coincidence that the earth is 70 percent water and so are our bodies! The Eastern cultures have more to teach us as Japanese researcher Masaru Emoto demonstrated some of the amazing properties of water with his water crystal research project. Emoto played music, displayed words, and prayed to water while it was freezing and once it was frozen, it created crystallized shapes that were distinct to each different stimulus. When the stimuli like the music and words were positive and loving, beautiful intricate shapes appeared, and when words and sounds were harsh or negative, more chaotic, distressed shapes appeared. Emoto is the author of *The Hidden Messages in Water* and postulates: What if we could use our thoughts and words for positive change when we are in water? Is it possible to rewire our bodies and minds and tap into the balance and peace it feels when in water? Intrigued by this concept, I decided to run a personal experiment to see what I could learn about connection and balance from water.

"Choose to be optimistic,
it feels better."

~ Dalai Lama

After six years of peaceful standup paddle boarding (SUP) on calm lakes, inlets, lagoons, and reservoirs across the country, I decided to take my SUP skills out to the ocean and hired someone to teach me how to paddle surf. Coincidentally, my instructor was just venturing out on her own to launch a new business focused on outdoor adventure instruction and I was her first client. It was only fitting that two people focused on learning from startups would meet on the water serendipitously to tackle this challenge together. It is through this trial-and-error lifestyle or "baptism by fire" approach that has taught me many great life lessons, so I expected this would be no different.

During my first surf lesson, I learned being present is the key to surfing. You must respect the ocean, or it will take you down. Paying attention to your board position, the current, what's below you and around you are all critical - and all at the same time. This is where and when multitasking finally wins! When you are distracted or if your back is to the current versus sideways, it's easy to become disoriented and miss navigating a rising swell which will knock you off your board. Sound familiar? When was the last time you didn't see that proverbial 2 x 4 coming toward your head that knocked you off balance? I should emphasize, I'm not SUP surfing because it is easier than regular surfing, but because I have prior SUP experience I thought would transfer and I'm already standing upright, which is metaphorically how we go through life. We stand tall as adults (posture is key!), hoping we don't get knocked over and bruise our egos. I have learned the sooner I drop my ego, the sooner I can learn what life can teach me.

While I expected that athletic ability would be most important, it is connection and balance in the water that drives a successful execution. To start, you paddle out past the surf to an area where you are level on the water standing on your board waiting behind the break. Then when the time is right, you begin to paddle slightly ahead of the swell, so as it rises, you can ride the wave and surf back to the shore. Following balance, patience is the next major factor since you do not paddle every swell. You wait….and you wait…and once you FEEL the connection to the water as the wave starts to build and roll, your intuition tells you to start paddling. It's a slower, more calculated process that requires you to be present and patient, so you can anticipate and feel what the water wants to do.

This is exactly what we need to learn and do; live connected in the present moment throughout life instead of operating on autopilot in a disconnected state.

Paddleboarding has also been teaching me about the transferability of skills. When learning how to SUP, you usually start in a lagoon, or a reservoir, which is relatively calm with your feet evenly spaced horizontally across the center of the board. I'm taking those skills to the ocean which I thought would help me keep my balance. One day when I fell off my board, which I'm used to, the plunge knocked something loose in my head. I came up from under the water, laughed and said to my instructor, "Hey, there's a really huge difference between the feel and connection of the water in the lagoon versus the ocean, and I don't have the footwork down to be able to move around on the board to navigate the swells here."

"What do you mean?" she asked.

"I'm bringing my lagoon skills to the ocean which doesn't transfer very well out here."

It was an aha! moment we both realized made perfect, logical sense as we are learning together through this process. She is learning how to transfer her knowledge and I'm learning how to apply it to my current skill set and the situation. I suggested we move closer into the shoreline where I could watch her first, then practice moving my feet and body on the board in the churn of the shallow water to get my balance, which is quite different from paddling in the lagoon. In life, how often do we show up with a tool set and we think we are going to do X, Y, and Z and that tool set is all we'll need to get the job done? We all have preconceived notions and expectations in our head, which often don't align with reality and create a teachable moment. The lesson here is to make sure you are building the right skills for the situation at hand before heading out into open seas.

I will close with this story about connection. Most of us have had many jobs throughout our lives. Some of them are more memorable than others for reasons completely unconnected to how that job relates to our past, current, or future career trajectory. In fact, on the face of it, some of the worst jobs I've had have been the most enjoyable because of the people. I think it has to do with alignment and working together towards the same goal, or perhaps it is just the sense of camaraderie that overrides the details of the actual job being done.

If the people are fun and the connections are good, you don't really care so much about the work you are doing. The summer after my first year in college, I sorted mail on the night shift at UPS. The reason I decided to accept this job was because in the morning I took a history class to fulfill a course credit, then I was lifeguarding in the afternoon. At 19, my reasoning was why not work a second job since I have the energy and that was good money for school! The one thing I failed to realize was that I actually needed to find some time in a 24-hour day to sleep.

From 10 p.m. to 2 a.m., I would sort mail into bins by zip codes with a group of women. We worked in a team of about ten because back then, men were hired to manage the big packages and drive the trucks and women sorted mail. We had this late-night hen circle spanning various ages and from all different walks of life, working this odd job for assorted reasons, and at the time it paid well -- $12 an hour in the late 80's. We were all open to working together as a team to meet the nightly package quotas as the time flew by. We laughed as we made up stories about the mail we were sorting, we learned about each other's lives, and we bonded in this strange, mundane, and nocturnal scenario. This odd summer job was one of the more memorable and enjoyable places I have worked. Why? Because it was about the connections to the people, not the actual job we did. This is not a suggestion to find a mindless job that pays well, but to take time to think about the connections that make doing anything we do worthwhile.

As I wrap up this chapter, the message I want to leave you with is that the connection to yourself is the most important. When you are in a bad place, when you're sick or you're unhappy, you may or may not want to connect with people. Learning to be our own best friend is the first step to be able to soothe and connect to ourselves before we can successfully connect with others. All these connections, and the Mihaly Csikszentmihalyi health benefits of them are critical to our well-being and our own ability to find balance.

KEY TAKEAWAYS

- If you feel you are living according to other's expectations, take a step back and examine what you really want. Figuring this out is a first step in the right direction.

- Making a conscious choice to be happy in each moment is taking your power back from letting outside forces and other people define you. Happiness is an inside job and despite all our grooming to the contrary, it is something within our control that leads to a state of positive being.

- Focus on your strengths and what comes naturally to you, so you are living in a positive state of being. Trying to be good at everything is a recipe for spreading your-self too thin, not being kind to yourself, and not honor-ing your unique talents.

- Once you get used to the idea of just being, you will become more in touch with your feelings and intuition. This will create better clarity around what wants to happen, and you will be more comfortable taking that inspired action – meaning just following your intuition as ideas and feelings surface.

- Start to pay more attention to what just feels right and trust your gut hunches. The more you experience the positive feedback that follows, the more this becomes a positive feedback loop over time and your confidence in your instincts will grow. Use them.

Chapter Four

Trust

"Knowing yourself is the
beginning of all wisdom."

~ Aristotle

Once upon a time there was a girl named Katie. She did everything right growing up in her midwestern family where her parents expected she would work hard to get good grades, naturally, to get into a good college to one day get a respectable job. It was what they had done, and they expected nothing less for their children. Katie had an older brother and a younger sister, and the same systems were in place for them. It was not onerous, or something that needed to be discussed. It was just a silent expectation. Her parents were not perfectionists and neither did they expect Katie to be, however, they always emphasized the importance of working hard to get ahead and Katie grew up with the belief that anything was possible for her in America. They expected she would have the same opportunities afforded her that her siblings did.

Katie graduated from high school with honors and a scholarship to attend a nearby state school that was well regarded. She was particularly interested in journalism and archaeology, but her father pointed out on more than one occasion that neither of those fields held much monetary promise for her, unless she wanted to spend her life teaching in academia. Katie's father had his own small accountancy firm, and her mother was a part-time social worker who did volunteer work in the community. So, Katie buckled down and eventually settled on a major in economics, even though she found it dry and boring. She did not come from a wealthy family and knew she was going to have to make her own way in the world as soon as she left college.

Right after she graduated, Katie got a job with a big accountancy firm in the city. With a starting salary of $50,000 she felt like she had made it. Her parents were both extremely proud of her and bragged about her success any chance they got. Katie wasted no time in furnishing her apartment with all the accoutrements of grown-up life now that she had a grown-up salary. Before she knew it, she was spending almost everything she earned, except for putting away 20 percent of each paycheck in her 401k, just like her parents encouraged her to do.

Yet, a growing sense of dissatisfaction gnawed at her with each passing quarter and each upwardly mobile promotion at her job. She could never make any sense of it because, by all external accounts, she had everything she wanted and could have hoped for – a good job, enough money to be saving for a down payment on a house, friends, and a social life. It wasn't that she hadn't met that special someone yet because she was in no hurry to get married and have kids. It was just that her first thought upon waking and usually last before sleeping went something along the lines of, "What's it all for?" or, "Is this it?" She felt a certain numbness. Nothing excited her. She thought maybe she needed to see a therapist, that perhaps something was wrong with her. When she tried, she was sent away with a clean bill of mental health which she shoved in her desk drawer back home.

One day in a bookshop, she stumbled upon Eckhart Tolle's book *The Power of Now*. It hit her like a lightning bolt, and she sat in the bookshop reading it until the store manager told her they were getting ready to close. She quickly paid for the book, took it home and finished it later that night. What Katie was coming to realize was that she had been living her entire life for other people, for their expectations of who she should be, do, and become. It was like the dominos began to fall when she discovered this life changing book. It then led her to other authors like Tony Robbins, Mike Dooley, and Joe Dispenza, along with innovative ideas she had never considered before. Within a few weeks she had signed up for a painting class at a local community center and a pottery throwing class in her neighborhood. She didn't know where it was all going to lead her, but she knew for the first time in a long time she felt alive again.

This is a fictional story. Katie could be any one of us. There are many of us who have followed the steps prescribed to us by family, school, or societal norms, only to wake up one day and wonder who we are or how we got to where we are. It is probably not hard for any of us to think of at least a few people we know who married the wrong person or followed a career encouraged or mandated by familial expectations.

We are taught to look outside ourselves for our missing pieces, rather than realizing much earlier in life that our north star is really inside. I am reminded of the Shel Silverstein children's book (although relevant for all ages!), *The Missing Piece Meets the Big O*. It's the story of the Missing Piece which sat alone, waiting for someone to come along and take it somewhere. All the Piece wanted was to roll along with its perfect match, but it couldn't find that match because they were either too small, too big, or some fit yet didn't roll. The Missing Piece felt sad and lonely until it met the Big O and learned from O that all it ever needed was to look inside for the support, encouragement, and determination to fulfill its dreams.

We are whole from birth ready to learn, and only seem to grow more splintered the further we march into adulthood with eager-eyed optimism to meet all the expectations around us. The same can be said about learning to trust ourselves. From an early age, we are rewarded for learning how to follow directions, how to sit quietly in our seats in class, to raise our hands to ask the teacher questions, then strive to produce the right answer. We are constantly fed a carrot and stick approach to life based on how our educational system has been set up since the middle of the 19th century.

Award winning teacher and author John Taylor Gatto took a hard look at the history of American education in his bestselling book, *Dumbing Us Down: The Hidden Curriculum of Compulsory Schooling*. When you look at how traditional school has been designed through the lens of history, as a one size fits all approach to training the working classes for a life of working in the factories on the manufacturing line, it all starts to make more sense. Gatto's thesis is that school was never meant to encourage and reward intellectual curiosity, but to teach students how to follow rules, to make children, and subsequently adults, emotionally and intellectually dependent upon authority. It encourages a kind of self-confidence that requires constant affirmation from outside sources (teachers, parents, partners, bosses, etc.) and teaches them that they cannot hide because they are always being supervised. Again, preparation for a life of factory work. Further, the dividing of children into age groups is more of a sorting mechanism that benefits school administrators and reinforces the idea of a class that one cannot escape, rather than having any meaningful output for the individual student or child.

There has been a movement in American education in the last 20-30 years to approach children more as individuals, but the system is so vast and entrenched in bureaucratic trappings, that it is difficult to truly affect change. There are always new bells and whistles to add to the curriculum that give teachers and administrators more hoops to jump through. Some of these approaches are Project-Based Learning or Harvard professor and author Howard Gardner's *Theory of Multiple Intelligences* that suggests that children have different ways of processing information and learning and that these ways can be independent of one another.

The theory is a critique of standard intelligence theory, which emphasizes the correlation between abilities and traditional metrics like IQ tests, which only consider linguistic, logical, and spatial abilities. Since 1999, Gardner has identified eight intelligences: linguistic, logical-mathematical, musical, spatial, physical/kinesthetic, interpersonal, intrapersonal, and naturalistic. Gardner and his colleagues have also considered two additional intelligences, existential and educational. Many teachers, school administrators, and special education teachers have been inspired by Gardner's theory of multiple intelligences, as it allowed for the idea that there is more than one way to define a person's intellect.

I am not criticizing his theory, or other novel approaches to teaching, because I believe they are trying to recognize that a one-size-fits-all approach to education no longer works. I'm suggesting that it is difficult to truly change an entrenched system that has been in existence for over 150 years and is based upon the standardization of learning that has children progress through its pathways according to a predetermined schedule. If they fail to keep up, they are then tracked into either being slow learners, and fed into a subsistence track, or fast-tracked into accelerated and advanced classes. To say I understand this problem is an understatement, because I lived it while I was in high school. As an incoming freshman, I was placed into an honors math track due to my seemingly odd high test score on a placement exam - math was never my strong suit. Despite tutoring and extra help outside of class, it was game on as I continued to struggle with honors algebra formula mastery. Even though I was failing consecutive semesters, a first for me, I watched my grades and my confidence deteriorate over the next two years as the school administrators debated my ability. "You just need to try harder!" they would say, and then tracked me into an honors geometry class the very next year. At age 15, what did I know? So, I tried harder, which only created more frustration. Since both my parents worked in education administration, guidance counseling specifically, you can imagine their actions were not a knee-jerk response when they began to dress for battle to win that war. To make matters more difficult for students experiencing what I did, evidence now shows that the pandemic and rise of Zoom learning across America has failed the students who were already struggling the most.[22]

Despite the progress made in the past decades in the realm of acknowledging that we do not all learn the same way, we are still beholden to an educational system that by and large is growing more outdated with every year that passes. In the past, it was a given that doing well in school prepared us for

---

[22] Meckler and Natanson. (2020). https://www.washingtonpost.com/education/students-falling-behind/2020/12/06/88d7157a-3665-11eb-8d38-6aea1adb3839_story.html

the coveted college education experience, or at least our parents thought it did, for us to get a decent job and become contributing members of society. Now, with a typical four-year college education, tuition is in the five digits and rising to six figures by the end of four years, and many families are rethinking whether it is all really worth it. With such revered institutions like MIT offering their full course offerings online for free, without the certification of a degree, many people are finding other ways to get the education they need. It is arguable that unless you need that actual B.A. or B.S. to go on to medical or law school, the value of that diploma might be negligible.

Young people are finding ways to stitch together an uncommon approach to education that involves experiential learning, internships, and online courses combined with time spent at community colleges or homeschooling. This allows them to transit faster through the system, earn the same degree at the end of it, all while spending a fraction of the cost along the way. I find this all very inspiring because people are taking ownership of their education and finding creative alternatives to a system that has grown stagnant and is failing to deliver on too many occasions.

Maya Frost, author of *The New Global Student: Skip the SAT, Save Thousands on Tuition, and Get a Truly International Education*, and her husband had four daughters in high school in 2005. They decided to sell everything and take their immediate family on an adventure living in South America, much to the horror of all their extended family and friends. What they found were numerous affordable, accessible, and amazingly advantageous options available to them that any American student can access to get a competitive global education. Their daughters all came back from their living abroad experience as either bi- or trilingual with an amazing education that enabled them to get into an assortment of international colleges around the world, all without ever actually taking the SAT or any other college prep test.

Closer to home, I have a friend in La Jolla, CA who did something similar with her family. She and her husband are educators and they decided to move to Costa Rica for several years with their middle school aged children to give them a wider lens on the world. The experiment offered their children expanded opportunities to learn with varying degrees of international experience and exposure. Now they are college bound with a much greater appreciation and ability to understand how the world works and all at a reduced cost. This proves the point that there are a multitude of ways to get a global education relevant for the 21st century that does not involve a one-size-fits-all standardized approach.

MINDSET AND GRIT

All these experiences would prepare anyone for having a "growth mindset," a term popularized in recent years in books like *Mindset* by Carol Dweck and *Grit* by Angela Duckworth. A growth mindset is, simply put, when an individual believes their talents and abilities can be developed through hard work, input from others, and by adopting strategies that can help them achieve more. Conversely, a person with a fixed mindset believes that their talents are intrinsic gifts they are born with that can neither be changed nor improved.[23]

It is not hard to see the benefits of having a growth mindset and how, in a world that is changing at such a rapid pace, we all must be responsible for our own growth and development whether it be in the personal or professional arena. There are misperceptions around exactly what a growth mindset is that Carol Dweck goes on to write about in the *Harvard Business Review*. "People often confuse a growth mindset with being flexible or open-minded or with having a positive outlook — qualities they believe they've simply always had. My colleagues and I call this a false growth mindset. Everyone is actually a mixture of fixed and growth mindsets, and that mixture continually evolves with experience."

People also think that a growth mindset is about praising and rewarding effort. In fact, outcomes matter and it is more productive to learn from outcomes that may sometimes be less than stellar or different than planned. This enables you to try different strategies or methods for meeting your desired outcomes. It is also not as simple as adopting a growth mindset as a way of being optimistic about the future. Dweck writes, "Organizations that embody a growth mindset encourage appropriate risk-taking, knowing that some risks won't work out. They reward employees for important and useful lessons learned, even if a project does not meet the original goals. They support collaboration across organizational boundaries rather than competition among employees or units. They are committed to the growth of every member, not just in words but in deeds, such as universally available development and

---

[23] Dweck. (2016). https://hbr.org/2016/01/what-having-a-growth-mindset -actually-means

advancement opportunities. And they continually reinforce growth mindset values with concrete policies."[24]

In Angela Duckworth's book *Grit*, she explores the idea that grit is a trait shared by the world's high achievers and she defines it as a combination of passion and perseverance for long-term goals. Duckworth believes that encouraging grit can particularly help adolescents and aligns with the ideas earlier in the chapter about expanding education beyond ticking the check boxes. Duckworth's research suggests that grit is not related to IQ but is closely related to conscientiousness. She also acknowledges there are other factors at play such as socioeconomic levers and environmental factors that enable individuals to succeed. "The question is not whether we should concern ourselves with grit or structural barriers to achievement. In the most profound sense, both are important, and more than that, they are intertwined."[25]

THE ENTREPRENEUR MYTH

The entrepreneur myth and ethos are deeply ingrained in American culture. Some would say it is the bedrock of our country since, if you think about it, once upon a time the country itself was a scrappy, break-away startup with big dreams and few resources. Our founding fathers and mothers were not deterred by obstacles and had a can-do attitude about building this country from the ground up.

Even today, innovation driven startups represent only two to three percent of all businesses, yet they create the majority

---

[24] Ibid.

[25] Duckworth. (2021). https://angeladuckworth.com/qa/#faq-63

of the revenue growth in our economy. The Bureau of Labor Statistics reports that over a recent three-year period, 34 percent of all private sector jobs were created by 80,000 high growth businesses.[26]

When I refer to the myth of the entrepreneur, it is not to discount the obvious spirit of entrepreneurship that is imbued in our country. In fact, it is the belief in the idea of limitless individual opportunity that fuels these ideals. According to the Case Foundation, which supports entrepreneurship and civic opportunity, it is "the belief that any individual—no matter their race, religion, gender, sexual orientation, economic background or geographic location—could bring their entrepreneurial talents to building the kinds of strong and diverse businesses and communities we need to keep our nation prosperous,"[27] that continues to fuel the obsession with entrepreneurship in America. But let's be honest, it is also the media frenzy we are constantly bombarded with every time a new startup goes public.

Again, the Case Foundation shines light on the fact that it is not a bed of roses for everyone and not all opportunities are created equal. Many of today's revered startups continue to be helmed and funded by "white, well-educated, and well-networked males."[28] While women or minority-led startups are growing at a faster rate than ever, they receive proportionally less investment than their white male counterparts. The foundation suggests the reason for this is not

---

[26] U.S. Bureau of Labor Statistics. (n.d.). https://www.bls.gov/

[27] Herrling. (2015). https://casefoundation.org/blog/the-myth-of-the -entrepreneur/

[28] Ibid.

that performance data is not on their side; in fact, diverse executive teams tend to have higher financial returns than their all-white male counterparts. It could be more that unconscious bias persists as humans, fallible that we are, tend to choose or favor people who look like them, think like they do or come from similar background and experiences as they do. Sadly, most angel investors still tend to be white males, however that demographic is also starting to change as more successful businesswomen try to shift that paradigm. According to data from the Angel Capital Association (ACA), just 22 percent of angel investors in the U.S. are women. In Europe, the situation is even more stark, with women amounting to just 14 percent of angel investors in the U.K. and 5 percent in France.[29] Companies like 37Angels and Citrine Angels in the Washington, D.C. area are working to change this demographic.

If we want to see expanded access to entrepreneurship in America, then the stories we share about it also need to change. By promoting more diverse stories around entrepreneurship, we can change the narrative and truly level the playing field.

LIMINAL THINKING

Liminal thinking is a term created by author Dave Gray who wrote a book by the same name. It is for people interested in creating change in their lives and starts with the premise that change is only possible by changing the way you think. Gray believes that we are both defined and limited by our belief

---

[29] Shuster. (2020). https://www.calcalistech.com/ctech/articles/0,7340,L -3799491,00.html

systems and that the only way out of that matrix is to change our fundamental belief systems. For example, if you want to quit smoking but fundamentally believe it is too hard, or for whatever reason like you don't want to or it is only something that some people can accomplish, chances are you will not be successful. If you examine the core belief underpinning around why you have failed to quit so far, you will have a better chance of succeeding when you try again. There is a beauty to this idea, and I realize it may sound deceptively simple.

The fact is, even if we don't realize it, we cling to our beliefs because they usually form our world view. According to Gray, we hold onto our beliefs like a lifeboat even if they are incomplete, invalid, or have grown obsolete. He created six principles around beliefs for people to examine:

1. **Beliefs are models** – They may seem like representations of the world, but they are fallible models for maneuvering a complicated, multidimensional, and ultimately unknowable reality.

2. **Beliefs are created** – We construct beliefs hierarchically, using theories and judgments, mostly from subjective personal experience.

3. **Beliefs create a shared world** – We use beliefs as psychological models to co-create a shared world we inhabit with others so we can live, work, and play together. To change this shared world requires changing the underlying shared beliefs.

4. **Beliefs create blind spots** – Holding onto beliefs can create blind spots which prevent us from seeing other possibilities.

5. **Beliefs defend themselves** – Beliefs are defended by a "bubble of self-sealing logic" which supports them to protect personal identity and self-worth.

6. **Beliefs are tied to identity** – "Governing beliefs" are the most difficult to change and deeply tied to personal identity and self-worth. You can't change these without changing yourself.[30]

Gray advises the reader to put the six principles into play via the following nine practices:

1. **Assume that you are not objective.** A lifetime of ingrained beliefs does not position you to be objective most of the time.

2. **Empty your cup.** Accept that you cannot learn new without letting go of old ideas and beliefs. Try to suspend judgment and remain open and curious where possible.

3. **Create a safe space.** People won't share their needs unless they feel it's safe, they will not be judged, and that they will be accepted.

4. **Triangulate and validate.** Adopt an open approach to looking at situations from a multitude of views. Consider new or contradictory beliefs.

5. **Ask questions, make connections.** Explore the social situation you're in to form new connections or find unexpected opportunities.

6. **Disrupt routines.** Many beliefs run on autopilot in the background of our lives. Disrupting routines and bringing unexpected insights to light.

---

[30] *Six Principles.* (2021). http://liminalthinking.com/six-principles/

7. **Act as-if in the here-and-now.** Act as if your belief is already true and see what happens. If it's working, do more of this to get the results you want.

8. **Make sense with stories.** Stories enable us to adopt new beliefs more easily than just a set of facts.

9. **Evolve yourself.** If you can tolerate change personally, this will enable you to create the future you want for yourself more easily. Be willing to be uncomfortable for a while.[31]

NEUROPLASTICITY

Recent advances in neuroscience have given rise to the term neuroplasticity, the ability of neural networks in the brain to reformat and change through growth and reorganization. These changes vary from individual neuron pathways making new connections, to systematic adjustments like cortical remapping. It's exciting because it means we can actually change our brains by changing our thoughts!

According to neuroscientist Dr. Rick Hanson's research, our brains are hardwired for negativity bias, but the good news is we change our wiring simply with conscious thought. This negativity bias means that the brain is exceptionally good at learning from bad experiences, but not as good at learning from good ones. Good experiences sort of bounce off the brain unfortunately, while bad ones make a deeper impression. This is the recipe he advises for rewiring our brain for positivity:

---

[31] Ibid.

HEAL YOURSELF

1. **H**ave a good experience – activate the experience.
2. **E**nrich this experience – help install this activated mental state into your brain and body.
3. **A**bsorb the experience – sense that it is sinking into you.
4. **L**ink the positive experience with something negative – the positive neurons will soothe the negative, then gradually replace them.

This is an exercise that is not meant to cover up negative truths. The more we take in the good, the more we're able to see the bad and do something constructive about it. This exercise will help dismantle the brain's stone age bias which obsessively focuses on the bad and worries about it.[32]

CORE VALUES

Taking time to examine our belief systems like David Gray suggests gives us a chance to explore and refine our core values. When we know our core values, we can see what belief systems are aligned and which ones are no longer serving our best interests, hopes, and dreams. Our values are central to our sense of identity, our sense of who we are, and our purpose. Values are the result of our deeply held convictions and shape our behavior and our decisions, big or small. When our

---

[32] Hanson. (2013). *Hardwiring Happiness: The New Brain Science of Contentment, Calm, and Confidence.*

external behavior does not match our internal values, we experience a disconnect, a separation between our head and our heart creating imbalance.

Core values grow out of decisions based on understanding what is really important to us and why they should come from a place of authenticity. Every choice we make strengthens our core values and who we are. Fully knowing, comprehending, and respecting our values propels our purpose and direction in life. Identifying and distilling our core values can be a road to deep and enduring satisfaction, joy, and meaningful contributions to our environments, whether they be the workplace, home, or greater community.

Some examples of core values you might identify could be self-sufficiency, freedom, optimism, curiosity, and simplicity. Take time and reflect on the aspects of life that are most important to you as your list will not look like someone else's. This will help you when you are faced with new choices and situations in your life because you will be able to use your list as a foundation to see how what you are evaluating aligns with your values. Blogger Omar Itani identifies some sample questions to ask yourself to make sure you are in alignment:

- If I do this, will I be staying true to myself?
- If I do this, will I be able to maintain my own self-sufficiency through it?
- What kind of impact will this have on others? Does that fulfill me?
- What effect will this have on my own well-being?

- Does this problem make me curious and am I interested in solving it? Is it something that will challenge me? Will it push me to expand and grow?[33]

Core values help you find alignment with your own truth, so you can learn how to trust your gut (your second brain!) and your heart in all that you do. If you don't have clarity around your core values, here is an exercise to help you identify them. Start by asking yourself, what beliefs do you have that may be holding you back from the life you really want to live?

A leader will find it difficult to articulate a coherent vision unless it expresses his core values, his basic identity...one must first embark on the formidable journey of self-discovery in order to create a vision with authentic soul.

~ Mihaly Csikszentmihalyi

---

[33] Itani. (2021). https://www.omaritani.com/blog/personal-values-and-intentional-living

FINDING YOUR TRUE NORTH

Values are principles, ethics, morals, standards, or those things that make up a code of behavior and can also be defined in terms of emotional states. During childhood, values develop and are influenced by our upbringing, families, life experiences, relationships, temperament, personality traits, education, etc. Our values may be so integrated into our internal operating system that we are not fully aware of them. Yet, they guide our lives, whether we realize it or not and influence our decisions and actions every day. When our values do not match our choices, obligations, and expectations (imposed by us or others), conflict results. When we fully understand our values and use them as a tool for making choices, we:

- Know why we want what we want.
- Make better decisions that fully resonate with who we are.
- Live with greater ease and less conflict.

TOWARD AND AWAY VALUES

There are "toward" values and "away" values. "Toward" values are the principles or emotional states that you would like to experience more often, i.e., the positive ones. Examples include love, connection, peace, excitement, adventure, freedom, and joy. "Away" values also impact our lives greatly, though they are things we would probably rather not experience and may not want to look at, e.g., pain, anguish, frustration, fear, loneliness, isolation, or shame.

THE EXERCISE

Through this activity you will come to fully understand your core values and learn to use them as a tool for making decisions in your life. First, list as many toward and away values as you can - target about 20 each. Do this **without** help from friends, spouses, partners, other family members, colleagues, etc. The assignment is yours to complete and is most powerful when the results come from only you, maybe with a little help from Google. Once you have a full list of both, edit and sort your list down to the top five that most resonate with you. Some people like to create a spreadsheet for this purpose, while others write them on post-its that can be moved around or just type a list.

Finally, take your top five choices of both toward and away values and complete one of these statements for each value for a total of ten statements.

Top 5 Toward

I can experience _____ every time I _____.

Top 5 Away

I only experience _____ when I _____ .

Once complete, save them somewhere so you can review them at least twice a year (Spring and Fall or New Year's and mid-Summer) to see if they need to be updated or changed for better alignment. This exercise is based on the work done by Northlight Coaching, which helps people find their true north through the Equine Gestalt Coaching Method®[34] using connection and experiential processing to create better life balance and personal peace.

KEY TAKEAWAYS

∾ Question conventional wisdom and anything you assume to be true without analyzing it from a critical perspective. Confirm that truth to be your own.

∾ Define what trust means to you and why it's important to create better alignment within your business and life. Share this information with those that matter to you.

∾ Ask yourself if you feel you are being held back by societal expectations or caught up in a belief system that is not yours. If so, work to realign your thinking toward your core values.

∾ Examine your beliefs and see if they are aligned with what you really want to achieve and if they aren't, challenge yourself to think differently and evolve them without judgement.

∾ Spend time figuring out or confirming your core values, then apply them to your decision-making process where and when you can.

---

[34] *Method.* (n.d.). https://www.northlightcoaching.com/method

Chapter Five

Failure

"If you're unwilling to taste failure,
there's no way on earth you can taste
the sweet fruits of your true potential."

~ Dr. Price Pritchett

I n my mid-twenties, after I had been working for a few years in marketing management roles for software startups, I decided it was a good idea to complete an MBA degree to help support my career path. At that time, MBA programs were in big demand as that piece of paper was, and still is, revered in the business world. Getting into any program would require all the check boxes properly ticked--and then some. It was this professional goal that would turn out to become one of my biggest lessons about failure, tenacity, and grit.

I was required to take the GMAT exam at that time for admission and standardized tests were never my specialty. While I am a very logical, common sense-based thinker, I pre-viously shared that grasping the realm of mathematical for-mulas was a challenge, so I worked hard to avoid them. Over the years I have learned to appreciate their role as they do serve a purpose despite my lack of proficiency.

After completing two GMAT prep courses, various sam-ple tests and two exams, my score did not meet the target, so admission was not granted despite my bachelor's degree, business management experience, driven work ethic, and past achievements. It was the first time in my life that I had to really think creatively to achieve a goal that seemed unattain-able. After several rejection letters and countless interviews with Admissions Deans at various schools, I took a break from beating my head against the wall. "If I just try harder, I know I can get in," I thought. Looking back, it was this pivotal expe-rience that absolutely was an invisible bridge to learning how to work "smarter not harder," as I call it. This situation helped me to understand that there is always another way to attack a problem, you just need to think differently to solve it and have the tenacity and grit to want to. Einstein said it best, insanity is doing the same thing repeatedly and expecting different results. Three years later, I completed my Master of Science in Management and graduated with honors, an achievement I am most proud of, especially after I was told by one Dean in particular that I didn't have what it takes to be successful in this type of program. Touché.

The following story is one of my favorites that I share often and is the epitome of creative problem solving. Author and speaker Dr. Price Pritchett wrote a parable about a fly to shine a light on struggle, failure, and success:

It's just past noon, late July, and I'm listening to the desperate sounds of a life-or-death struggle going on a few feet away. There's a small fly burning out the last of its short life's energies in a futile attempt to fly through the glass of the windowpane. The whining wings tell the poignant story of the fly's strategy—try harder. But it's not working. The frenzied effort offers no hope for survival. Ironically, the struggle is part of the trap. It is impossible for the fly to try hard enough to succeed at breaking through the glass. Nevertheless, this little insect has staked its life on reaching its goal through raw effort and determination. This fly is doomed. It will die there on the windowsill.

Across the room, ten steps away, the door is open. Ten seconds of flying time and this small creature could reach the outside world it seeks. With only a fraction of the effort now being wasted, it could be free of this self-imposed trap. The breakthrough possibility is there. It would be so easy. Why doesn't the fly try another approach, something dramatically different? How did it get so locked in on the idea that this particular route, and determined effort, offer the most prom-ise for success? What logic is there in continuing, until death, to seek a breakthrough with "more of the same"?

No doubt this approach makes sense to the fly. Regretta-bly, it's an idea that will kill.

"Trying harder" isn't necessarily the solution to achieving more. It may not offer any real promise for getting what you want out of life. Sometimes, in fact, it's a big part of the prob-lem. If you stake your hopes for a breakthrough on trying harder than ever, you may kill your chances for success.[35]

Haven't we all been that fly at some point in our lives? Flapping our wings to no avail? Trying all the same methods without luck in pursuit of our goals? Beating our head over and over against that solid metaphorical window that simul-taneously shows us our freedom, but then prevents us from achieving it? Failure is part of life and can become a best friend if you let it teach you something new.

Dr. Edith Ava Eger, author of *The Choice*, suffered unspeak-able tragedies during the Holocaust in World War II. She lost her family in the concentration camps, was forced to dance in front of Nazi concentration camp doctor Josef Mengele to prove her worth and didn't find any safety until she escaped and reached Georgia in the United States. Yet her book is not a memoir, nor a plea for empathy. It is more of a guide on how to turn tragedy or failure into fuel for an optimistic life, so you can make the best lemonade possible and maybe add a splash of Titos! Dr. Eger went on to become a therapist and special-ized in helping people recover from several types of traumas. You could say she was a learned expert, notwithstanding her

---

[35] Pritchett. (n.d.). https://www.pritchettnet.com/you2

educational credentials. She believes that if you choose an optimistic outlook on life, reality will follow suit. In essence, if we reframe our failures or traumas as learning experiences, it enables us to choose love and success over hate or failure.[36] If the fly had been able to make a different choice and try something new, he might have survived.

By now, we have all heard the often-repeated stories of how Steve Jobs was fired from Apple at thirty years old or how Oprah Winfrey was fired from her news anchor job and was told she would never have a career in TV. Then there is the fact that Albert Einstein failed primary school and Michael Jordan was cut from his high school basketball team. Lucille Ball was told she was talentless (despite her ability to eat a lot of chocolates) and should leave drama school. JK Rowling, a single parent on welfare, was rejected by publishers dozens of times before someone recognized her brilliance. Daniel Craig slept on park benches early in his career while trying to break into acting and couldn't find work – yes, James Bond was temporarily homeless. The list goes on and probably could fill the Taj Mahal. Nevertheless, when it comes to experiencing and even welcoming personal failure closer to home, we still cringe and the prospect of it usually keeps us from even trying something new at all. Yoda said it best, *"Do or do not. There is no try."*

It's easy and fun to read about failure when it comes to *other people* but when it's ours, or our loved ones, not so much. As we discussed in the last chapter about how our educational system shapes us from an early age, it definitely steers us away

---

[36] Bernstein. (2019). https://offtheshelf.com/2019/04/the-choice-by-edith -eva-eger/

from having a healthy tolerance for failure. Being expected to always give the right answers, achieve the best grades, or gain successful admission into a reputable college doesn't always encourage design thinking.

Failure has been getting better press in recent years as these anecdotes of iconic failures, followed by later successes, infiltrate our cultural consciousness. It is easy to dismiss these stories as things that happen once in a blue moon or as black swans, the term coined by author Nicholas Naseem Taleb for huge, unexpected events that are later explained by looking back at history, but which seemingly no one was able to predict. Examples of black swans are 9/11 and the 2008 banking crisis.[37]

It is important to examine failure because it will teach you how to survive and thrive outside of your comfort zone. This valuable skill will help create an open mind to try new things, like the ideas in this book for a more balanced life. The measure to which we are willing to embrace and even welcome our failures is proportionate to the upside we can gain from the lessons that failure will teach us – **if** we are willing to listen and learn. Rationally, we could all agree with the idea that to live in fear of trying to pursue what our heart desires, is in fact, no way to live. That is, however, how many of us pass our days. We would rather accept the steady paycheck than take that risk of starting our own business or selling all our possessions and becoming a digital nomad, exploring the country in an RV, untethered by mortgages, utility bills, and PTA meetings.

---

[37] Taleb. (2010). *The Black Swan: The Impact of the Highly Improbable.*

I have not failed. I've just found 10,000 ways that won't work.

~ Thomas Edison

What is the biggest component in learning to accept and even welcome failure? I believe it is bravery. According to speaker and author of *The Ascent of Humanity*, Charles Eisenstein, "Bravery means doing what is yours to do, when it is time to do it. Denying that knowing locks your heart in a box. Life becomes a chore. Despair descends like a fog, turning everything gray. Hope withers, leaving behind the dry empty husk called wishful thinking. And you face the dread of living the rest of life knowing, 'I did not do what I was here to do, when the moment came, and it counted."[38]

Bravery is often associated with speaking up, taking a stand, or singling oneself out from the crowd in some other way to be the other, lone voice. We cannot forget that bravery applies to our personal choices as well – whether to step away from the expectations of those around us when it comes to our calling in life or simply our current job, what we study, who we love, being able to declare our personal preferences despite our fear of rejection. Being brave means not living under a shroud of who we are supposed to be – like the gay teenager who comes out to their staunchly religious parents. He hopes they will not reject him, but he is willing to do it anyway because even at his young age, he knows he will live a life of lies otherwise.

---

[38] Eisenstein. (2013). *The Ascent of Humanity*.

It is interesting that even the word failure is defined by a negative, an absence of something. The Merriam-Webster Dictionary defines it as "omission of occurrence or performance" and as "a state of inability to perform a normal function."[39] We can take lessons from failure in a number of ways. The first being we can use it as a reality check to take stock of where we are and what we need to do to achieve our goals. What changes do we need to make that might lead to an outcome that we would consider *not* a failure?

When they say failure is the greatest teacher, they weren't kidding. Sometimes our failures are in the public eye, like an athlete fumbling the ball during a game or an actor missing their cue on the stage. Other times, that failure is held within a tighter circle, like a mishandled business deal, a delayed project roll out or an epic disappointment at home. When these things do not go according to plan, it will give you a chance to examine what went wrong and learn what you can do differently next time. Luckily, you also rarely get one shot at something. Steven Spielberg had to apply to UCLA Film school several times before he got in. If you fail the first time, learn from it, apply the lessons, and try again.

The other less tangible but no less important aspect of failure is that it helps build grit and tenacity, like we discussed earlier. Consider failure a gift because, trust me, it builds character. You will find out what you are made of. If it's regular oatmeal, it will give you a chance to make steel cut oats instead. You can also use failure as a force for motivation. Sylvester Stallone had his script *"Rocky"* rejected over 1,500 times

---

[39] *Failure.* (n.d.). https://www.merriam-webster.com/dictionary/failure

before he finally found a deal. Alice Darnell profiles his story in her blog about failure:

Sylvester Stallone had it rough as a child, being taunted in school and constantly in and out of foster homes. As an adult, things didn't improve as he was unable to earn a steady income, and even had to sell his dog for $25.00 to help pay his electricity bill. It was only 2 weeks after selling his dog that he wrote the Rocky script in nearly 20 hours straight. After being rejected over 1,500 times (that's more than Edison's failure!), Stallone was given a nod by United Artists for $125,000... but only if Stallone would not star in it. Stallone refused. Even when he was subsequently offered $250,000 and $325,000, he still refused as he wanted to star in it. He finally reached a compromise, starring in the film but only taking $35,000 and a percentage of profits as a concession. What was Stallone's first purchase with his $35,000? His beloved dog, for $15,000! But I am sure he could afford it seeing as Rocky grossed over $200,000,000 and his sequels grossed over a billion dollars![40]

The hit film *Good Will Hunting* was written and produced by Matt Damon and Ben Affleck. At the time, they were complete unknowns in Hollywood and couldn't get any producers or studios to finance their film or take them seriously. The two young actors taking that huge risk and producing their film themselves turned out to not only be their big break but created a movie that became widely acclaimed.

Sometimes risk and failure can appear in more subtle ways. In a recent article from the Harvard Business Review, it revealed that leaders who have an over emphasis on efficiency

---

[40] Dartnell. (n.d.). https://www.lifehack.org/articles/work/6-benefits-failure-that-proove-that-actually-good-thing.html

and productivity can wind up being less effective because they spend less time being people focused. "The result is often a negative impact on organizational climate and burnout of team members. In a 2017 study by Kronos and Future Workplace, burnout was highlighted as the biggest threat to employee engagement, with 95 percent of HR leaders citing it as a key driver of employee turnover."[41] Our post pandemic work culture absolutely underscores this statistic and I have definitely experienced this management style during my career.

This aligns with the overarching message of this book, which is about the need for balance as leaders, executives, and quite simply, as people. The point of the HBR article is that leaders can often 'fail' by being too good in one area. Many leaders neglect focusing on relationships and morale building, which can have long-term negative costs for a company such as high employee turnover. The article goes on to share that leaders who are not over-focused on tasks or productivity, and prioritize relationships and morale building, are more able and willing to "go slow to go fast" and can do so while keeping the broader needs of the enterprise in mind. Conversely, task-focused leaders more often tend to be highly directive, controlling or perfectionistic which more often leads to feelings of alienation or lack of autonomy and ownership among teams.

In these instances, failure can be subjective and open to interpretation. Perhaps the end of quarter results are good in monetary terms, but if there is high employee turnover and

---

[41] Zucker. (2019). https://hbr.org/2019/02/why-highly-efficient-leaders-fail

massive dissatisfaction throughout the company – how successful is that company really and who wants to work there?

The most important takeaway here is that failure is all about the framing we do in our minds. In life, there is always the "thing" that happens – then what we decide to do or feel or think about it, and these are the things that are always within our control. We may not be able to control all outcomes, but the story we tell ourselves about them most certainly is. As the saying goes, *the comeback is always greater than the setback*, which is a mindset.

> "The impediment to action advances action. What stands in the way becomes the way."
>
> ~ Marcus Aurelius

Let's look to the Stoic philosophers for some useful lessons about failure. The ancient wisdom of Stoicism began in the early 3rd century BC. Founded in Athens by Zenon de Citium, Stoicism was embraced by some of our early American founders like George Washington and Benjamin Franklin. Over time, we lost sight of this philosophy and it was no longer discussed or spoken about in our classrooms. The essence of what it means to be a Stoic is accepting that we can't control and can't rely on outside events or things for our happiness or peace of mind. Instead, we must gain our wisdom through applying the principles of Stoicism to practice a better outlook, self-awareness, and way of life.

The Stoics were fond of practicing "negative visualization" – reviewing the many scenarios in their minds that could go wrong. They did this mainly so they could go into any situation and remove the element of surprise. According to The Daily Stoic, "The wise man is aware of all possibilities and prepared for all of them. In this way, there is no such thing as failure – simply outcomes."[42] Seen this way, failure is simply a chance – an invitation to get better.

I have a friend who seems to be eternally stuck in life. She has a decent job as a fundraiser for a large, high-profile charity where she holds a senior position. She has been complaining about her job for years, which she knows she does well, but she never feels like her work is appreciated or valued. She talks about all the things she would like to try and do, yet never does them. There is always a reason, always an excuse. Yet the complaining and dissatisfaction doesn't stop. We probably can all think of a person like this we know or have known in our lives. My theory is my friend's fear of failure is keeping her locked in a prison of her own mind. Rather than trying and finding out what new frontiers might have in store for her where she can use her special talents for good to the fullest and feel productive, instead she does nothing.

Truly, the more you embrace failure, the more it will lose its grip on you as any immobilizing force, keeping you from doing or trying the things you really want to in life. If you fail, it means you tried. As Winston Churchill famously said, "Success consists of going from failure to failure without loss of

---

[42] *A Stoic Response to Failure.* (n.d.). https://dailystoic.com/stoic-response -failure/

enthusiasm." And let's not forget, he also said, "You create your own universe as you go along."

KEY TAKEAWAYS

- **Redefine failure.** Make a list of what went wrong in your most recent experience of failure and see what you can learn and tweak to try differently next time.

- **Share your failures.** Share stories at work about your own personal failures. Show people it's okay to try – and to fail. Leading by example will help others move forward after failure and learn from it.

- **Create a failure award.** Do this for yourself, for your family, for your team at work, and make it fun. Reward the courage to try something that didn't work, then discuss and learn from it.

- **Keep an open mind.** Shift your mindset to see mistakes as a teachable moment. Trial and error along with failure is the best teacher since hindsight is 20/20. This will help reframe perceived failures into a series of different and possible outcomes to learn from.

- Don't beat yourself up over past mistakes, learn from them then let them go. The more you are forgiving and kind to yourself, the more you will be present in the moment.

Chapter Six

Karma

"You must be the change you
wish to see in the world."

~ Mahatma Gandhi

have a good friend who used to own property in Orange Beach, Alabama, a beautiful coastal spot on the tip of the Pensacola panhandle. She and her wife owned a lovely townhouse, steps away from the beach, in a row of six that were attached. Because they operated as their own little community, they decided to work together and created their own housing association (HOA) to help keep each other accountable and split costs associated with managing their beachfront oasis.

The man who lived in the last unit on the end wanted to do his own thing and not support the group, nor did he sign the housing association paperwork. Clearly, he never watched Sesame Street and was that kid who made the unpopular choice to do his own thing regardless how it affected everyone else. He even fought the rest of the neighbors tooth and nail on every proposed decision for the community, such as making the units as hurricane proof as possible. When Hurricane Ivan ripped through the area in 2004 and took no prisoners, many properties were impacted and there was a lot of clean up that needed to be done. The other five households worked together to fix the extensive damage and split the cost. What happened to the sixth one who would have nothing to do with the group to improve the community? Well, he fought the cleanup efforts and tried to sue the HOA to cover his damages. Instead of making it to court to explain his case, he had a massive heart attack, died, and his unit went into foreclosure with the local bank. True story.

Just as we have the opportunity to choose our response to failure, we have the opportunity to put good energy out into the world, which can be viewed as karma. Think of that friend or neighbor who is always complaining about something and how the world seems to be pitted against them. What do they seem to get in return for possessing an outlook like Pigpen in the Charlie Brown cartoon series – the one who walks through life with a 'rain cloud' of dirt above his head? More of the same and then some.

WHAT IS KARMA?

Karma is an ancient Indian religious concept based on the idea that our words, deeds, and actions in this life have a direct effect on our next life, or even in the future of our current lives. Essentially, "good intent and good deeds contribute to good karma and happier rebirths, while bad intent and bad deeds contribute to bad karma and bad rebirths."[43] In many schools of Indian religions especially Hinduism, Buddhism, Jainism and Sikhism, as well as in Taoism, the philosophy of karma is intricately linked to the idea of rebirth. In these schools of thought, karma in the present affects one's future in the present life, as well as the nature and quality of the future life – or one's saṃsāra.[44] This concept has also been adopted in popular Western culture, where events that occur after a person's actions can be seen as natural consequences.

A simple and eloquent description of karma comes to us from Deepak Chopra's website: "Karma is energy, which in itself is neither good nor bad; these are just the labels people choose to attach to it. The energy created by an action has to be

---

[43] Halbfass. (2000). *Karma und Wiedergeburt im indischen Denken.*
[44] "Karma." (1997). The Concise Oxford Dictionary of World Religions.

returned: 'As yea sow so shall yea reap.' It cannot be avoided. When you perform an action, it creates a memory, which in turn generates a desire, which leads you to perform another action. For example: You take your first yoga class (action), then you know what happens in a yoga class (memory), and if you enjoyed the class, you decide to go back the following week (desire), and that following week you turn up again with your mat (action). Karma creates memories and desires, which then determine how you live. Actions, memories, and desires are the Karmic software that run your life."[45]

Whether you subscribe to the ancient Indian philosophy and religious views of life that suggest that karma is part of the reincarnation process and the deeds you sow in one life are reaped in the next is not of the most importance. What the idea of karma can yield to us is that we are continually creating our own lives, here and now. We don't need to be trapped hamsters on the wheel of life, chasing endlessly in the same cycles to nowhere. We can break out of our habits and patterns and create the life we really want to be leading anytime.

According to Chopra, we do not need to be doomed to a life of paying for past mistakes, but we can take steps to improve the quality of our current actions, which can help us either improve or transcend karma. His suggestions for ways to do this include:

Making Conscious Choices – Making good choices can lessen the intensity or magnitude of situations that arise from returning karma. Also, the quality of your current

---

[45] Gabriel. (2016). https://chopra.com/articles/how-does-karma-affect -your-life

choices affects your future karma. Ask yourself if these choices are good not only for you, but those around you.

Be Forgiving – It is possible to forgive a person without forgiving the act. Being able to forgive is part of spiritual growth. From the vedantic perspective, all hurts we experience are the result of some karma.

Cultivate Gratitude – When you start practicing gratitude for all positive things in your life, expect to see more of the same show up. (Oprah swears by this!)

Seek Growth – As discussed in earlier chapters, having a growth mindset allows one to view failure or other challenging circumstances as opportunities to grow, change, and do better next time. Embracing growth enables us to move forward on our karmic journey.

Discover your Dharma – Dharma is your true purpose or truth in life. When you find this and are living in alignment with this, your actions will "spontaneously correct," and you won't even create karma.

Meditate – Here it is. You've heard it before. According to Chopra, this is the most powerful tool we have in our arsenal to help us on our spiritual path. Try to view meditation as simply a move away from activity into silence. Try using mantras to help you turn down the dial of buzz and activity in your brain. It's not about trying to empty your mind, but to sit with yourself and be aware and present in the moment. "Meditation realigns you with your true self, leads you back to your true purpose (Dharma) and allows you to 'wash' away Karma on all levels."[46]

"Watch your thoughts, they become your words; watch your words, they become your actions; watch your actions, they become your habits; watch your habits, they become your character; watch your character, it becomes your destiny."

~ Lao Tzu

NEW AGE THOUGHT AND SCIENCE

There are numerous ways one can view karma, or decision-making, if you prefer. Both science and new age thought give us ample opportunities to find connections from disparate ends of the spectrum.

At this point, most of us are familiar with the Law of Attraction as a woo-woo idea from the 2006 hit movie *The Secret*. In fact, the Law of Attraction has been around a lot longer than that. The concept was first introduced in 1906 by author William Walker Atkinson who wrote *Thought Vibration or the Law of Attraction in the Thought World*. He introduced concepts of thought, energy, vibration, and manifestation to readers

---

[46] Ibid.

who likely had not encountered such radical ideas before. A few years after that came the publication of the early self-help book, *The Science of Getting Rich* by Wallis D. Wattles. He also was an early purveyor of the concept of gratitude in getting what one wanted out of life. By 1928, Napoleon Hill published his first book, *The Law of Success in 16 Lessons*, which referred to the Law of Attraction several times. A few years later, came his more famous classic, *Think and Grow Rich*.

This background points to the fact that these ideas and concepts have been around for quite some time. The basic tenet of the Law of Attraction is that our positive thoughts and creative visualizations create the reality that we desire and envision for ourselves, which may come as a surprise, but dovetails with the tenets of quantum physics.

Quantum mechanics is the branch of physics that deals with the infinitesimally small, leading to some very mind-blowing conclusions about the physical world. On the atomic and electronic scale, many of the equations in classical mechanics describe how things move at everyday speeds and sizes lose their usefulness. In classical, Newtonian mechanics, objects exist at a specific time in a specific place. In quantum mechanics, however, objects exist instead in the haze of probability; they have one chance of getting to point A, another chance of getting to point B, and so on.

Quantum mechanics (QM) evolved over many decades and began as a series of controversial mathematical explanations of experiments that the mathematics of classical Newtonian mechanics could not explain. It began in the early 20th century, about the time that Einstein published his theory of relativity, a separate mathematical revolution in physics that describes the motion of things at high speeds. Unlike Einstein's theory of relativity, the origins of QM cannot be attributed to a single scientist. Instead, a number of scientists contributed to the founding of the main principles of QM that were gradually accepted and experimentally verified between 1900 and 1930.

Later in the 20th century, British physicist David Bohm expanded on Einstein's early theories even further. Bohm was committed to understanding the nature of reality and consciousness as a coherent whole, which he theorized was constantly evolving. Bohm's thesis was that the old mechanistic-Newtonian-Cartesian view of the universe which implied that mental and physical are separate was far too limited. He believed that thought is distributed and non-local just as quantum particles are. His reasoning expanded the understanding of quantum physics from the scientific world into the social and humanistic aspects of society, saying that our traditional view of the division of the mental and physical led to unnecessary and troubling divisions in society. He also developed the theory that the brain operates more as a hologram, more like quantum mathematical principles and the properties of wave patterns.

Bohm published his seminal *Wholeness and the Implicate Order* in 1980. He suggested that beneath underlying physical appearances, or what he deemed the "explicate order," there is a deeper, hidden "implicate order." He applied this theory to the quantum realm and proposed that the implicate order is a field holding an infinite number of fluctuating pilot waves. When these waves overlap, we observe particles, which make up the explicit order. He hypothesized that even space and time may be manifestations of a deeper, implicate order.

To delve further into the implicate order, Bohm suggested that physicists might need to do away with basic assumptions about nature. During the Enlightenment, Newton and Descartes replaced the ancients' organic concept of order with a more mechanistic view. Bohm wanted scientists to eventually move beyond the mechanistic and even mathematical paradigms of the universe. "We have an assumption now that's getting stronger and stronger that mathematics is the only way to deal with reality. Because it's worked so well for a while, we've assumed that it has to be that way."[47]

Bohm predicted that one day, science and art will merge. He said that, "This division of art and science is temporary, it didn't exist in the past, and there's no reason why it should go on in the future."[48] He believed that people's ability to perceive and think differently far outweighs the simple accumulation of knowledge.

How does this all relate to the day to day of our lives and finding balance? It is just further proof that the reality we choose to create is very much within our control. And, like the Stoics, we can choose our response to the events that are outside of our control, as Dr. Esther Eger did when reframing the traumas of her life to not only survive but thrive.

We are seeing increasing instances of spirituality overlapping with science over the last several decades. You could even say that Dr. Eger is the spiritual side of quantum physics.

Olympians and other professional athletes have long been using visualization in their training to help them achieve

---

[47] Bohm in Horgan. (2018). https://blogs.scientificamerican.com/cross -check/david-bohm-quantum-mechanics-and-enlightenment/
[48] Ibid.

successful outcomes.[49] It is so common to use this skill that is never questioned or viewed as alternative or woo-woo. Yet when we suggest that 'normal' people do the same in their lives, it is still considered a bit out of the ordinary. Try taking a page from your favorite professional athlete and rehearse the outcome you desire – imagine it as specifically as you can, right down to using every sense in your body to feel it and bring it to life in your mind. The good news is you don't have to be Michael Phelps to do it.

"Every great dream begins with
a dreamer. Always remember,
you have within you the strength,
the patience, and the passion to reach
for the stars to change the world."

~ Harriet Tubman

The crux of this chapter is to show you how our thoughts create your reality and that creating the outcomes we want is very much within our control. If you are grounded in your own truth and core values, then you are one step closer to being in alignment. There are, however, other ways to both find and foster alignment in your life.

---

[49] Burroughs. [Video]. (n.d.). https://olympics.com/en/video/can-imag-ining-success-actually-help-you-achieve-it-olympic-state-of-mind?ux-reference=playlist

When you feel energized by purpose, then you are on the path of alignment. Sometimes we may not immediately know what that purpose is, but by following our inclinations, our instincts, our intuition, or our gut, then we find it. This example has been used countless times in the field of personal development, but it bears repeating. If you think back to when you were about 10 or 12 years old, remember what you loved more than anything at that time. Okay, leaving aside doughnuts or Saturday morning cartoons, there are often clues to what still excites you as an adult. It is a good starting point for finding our purpose. If we can spend at least part of each day pursuing what lights us up, even if it's after everyone else has gone to bed in your house and you're taking an hour for yourself to engage in some right-brained creative activity you love like painting, dancing in your kitchen or working on your next novel, that is a step in the right direction.

If you find yourself using a lot of drugs, alcohol, food, or any other substance to continually avoid dealing with things in your life, then that is an obvious sign that you are out of alignment. Rituals and routines can help us find our way back to a balanced lifestyle. Simply creating both a morning and an evening ritual can help bookend your day and keep you grounded.

When you find yourself ready to ditch habits that no longer serve you, you can be sure that you are on a path to creating better life balance. It is why some people seek out military training to create structure, and a sense of purpose or balance in their life.

Life starts to feel easier when you are in alignment with your purpose and less like you are pushing a boulder up a mountain. You are able to trust and surrender to the Universe (or God, or whatever higher power works for you) that you are supported, and it has your back. In Gabrielle Bernstein's book *The Universe Has Your Back*, she offers Universal Lessons, stories, life examples and practical steps to help transform fear to faith to live your best life and reclaim your personal power. She writes, "The answer is to lead from a place of love. Our capacity to tune in to the energy of love gives us the words we need when we're ready to speak up, the compassion we need when it's time to forgive, and the power we need when we are lost. As a spiritual activist, I believe that the greatest power we have to combat the terror of these times is our power to live in love. Love casts out all fear."[50]

When you lead from a place of love, you will also find that people around you are generally nicer too. The saying "your vibe attracts your tribe" exists for a reason. You will find yourself more easily able to avoid negative energy in your life and naturally attract those in alignment with your positive energy as we already discussed how like attracts like. You might even find that the golf gods have compassion, too, and grant you that hole-in-one you have been waiting patiently for or that your guardian angel shows up to support you on a more regular basis. Like when you are randomly presented with just the right parking spot in front of the entrance where you are going at just the right time to make it to your target destination - early. We all have that guide or guardian angel looking out for us and maybe even met her at some point over the course of our lives, even fleetingly, as there are no coincidences in life.

---

[50] Bernstein. (2016). *The Universe Has Your Back.*

When you are in alignment, your manifestations of your dreams and purpose start to show up more regularly in a synchronistic fashion. As I said, whether you are religious or just consider yourself spiritual, or even just spiritually curious, you have probably at one time or another said to yourself, "Could I just have a sign I'm on the right track?" This is your yearning for alignment making itself known to you. We have all wanted a proverbial metaphysical 'thumbs up' when we are feeling stuck or frustrated. Sometimes all we have to do is ask for a sign, and then there it is when we are dialed into the present moment, connected, and paying attention. Now, you can argue that it is nothing more than us answering our own questions by assigning meaning to things that are basically meaningless. Go for that interpretation if you must. I'm not going to hold you back. But isn't it a bit like a cat chasing its tail? Where the meaning comes from – whether it is God or a little green creature next to a spaceship, is probably less important than the meaning it provides us.

The truth is, we are sent signs all the time, but we don't acknowledge them, or we ignore them, or we simply downplay their meaning and dismiss them as pure coincidence. Carl Jung coined the term *synchronicity* to describe a meaningful coincidence of two or more similar or identical events that are causally unrelated. Jung told the following story as an example:

By way of example, I shall mention an incident from my own observation. A young woman I was treating had, at a critical moment, a dream in which she was given a golden scarab. While she was telling me this dream I sat with my back to the closed window. Suddenly I heard a noise behind me, like a gentle tapping. I turned around and saw a flying insect knocking against the windowpane from outside. I opened the window and caught the creature in the air as it flew in. It was the nearest analogy to a golden scarab that one finds in our latitudes, a scarabaeid beetle, the common rose-chafer (Cetonia aurata), which contrary to its usual habits had evidently felt an urge to get into a dark room at this particular moment.

It was an extraordinarily difficult case to treat, and up to the time of the dream little or no progress had been made. I should explain that the main reason for this was my patient's animus, which was steeped in Cartesian philosophy and clung so rigidly to its own idea of reality that the efforts of three doctors—I was the third—had not been able to weaken it. Evidently something quite irrational was needed which was beyond my powers to produce. The dream alone was enough to disturb ever so slightly the rationalistic attitude of my patient. But when the "scarab" came flying in through the window in actual fact, her natural being could burst through the armor of her animus possession and the process of transformation could at last begin to move.[51]

When a synchronicity happens to you, it won't have meaning for anyone else. That is the point – they are particular to you, your circumstances, and your journey. If you are still not convinced, just recognize and use these signs when they happen to you as reminders to keep you focused on achieving your goals and dreams.

Remember how your mother, or grandmother, used to say to you, "You catch more bees with honey than you do vinegar"?

---

[51] Jung. (1969). *Synchronicity: An Acausal Connecting Principle.*

These are cliches and phrases we laugh at growing up but as we grow older, we recognize the wisdom in them. I believe it's just another example of karma at work.

Let's apply the Law of Attraction to business. If we go back to the idea that like attracts like, you will be more likely to bring people, events, and circumstances into your life that resonate with your vibe and aspirations. It works both ways, of course. Be the positive force you want to be in the world, and you will seem the same reflected back to you.

Look at the glass half full and believe that your success is inevitable. The Law of Attraction suggests that you decide what you want but leaves the mechanics of how you will get it to the Universe, or higher power, or God. Think of it just like you are ordering from Amazon -- you place your order and then trust they will logistically arrange for your package to be delivered. Most people who have achieved amazing successes didn't necessarily know the details of how they were going to do it, they just trusted that, somehow, they would. Try doing an experiment where you walk around for a day behaving as if a thing you want is already yours. You don't have to tell any-one you are doing this in case you're embarrassed about being so presumptuous. It's a thought exercise and doesn't cost you anything but can bring you closer to your desired outcomes based on the energy and focus you are putting on your intent.

This is not to suggest you should loll around imagining remarkable things happening to you and not doing anything about them. You still need to take inspired action, do what feels right towards your outcomes, but don't try to get there by driving a round peg into a square hole. Don't be afraid to dream big and don't let anyone tell you that you shouldn't. The cliché, "Rome wasn't built in a day," was coined for a reason. Great, big dreams can take time to manifest. Don't give up on them.

I want to close this chapter by encouraging you to think about your choices – are you grounded in your intuition and aligned with your core values when you are making them? When you can do that, you will most certainly be creating better karma for yourself, whether for this life or the next, if that's how you roll. Plus, why not try, it feels better too!

THOUGHTS ARE THINGS

You can never tell what your thoughts will do
In bringing you hate or love,
For thoughts are things, and their airy wings
Are swift as a carrier dove.
They follow the law of the universe -
Each thing must create its kind -
And they speed o'er the track to bring you back
Whatever went out from your mind.

Ella Wheeler Wilcox[52]

---

[52] Wheeler Wilcox. (n.d.). http://www.ellawheelerwilcox.org/poems/ptthings.htm

KEY TAKEAWAYS

～ Identify what is really important to you and focus on it with fierce intent. Be brutally honest with yourself and don't let past failures or disappointments hijack your dreams.

～ Focus on gratitude daily and getting into a regular practice of positive self-talk. Science has proven optimism leads to more positive outcomes, so keep your glass half full.

～ Be mindful and intentional with your words. Communicate with others the way you hope to be communicated with as words are powerful and can't be taken back.

～ Visualize success. See it as if it has already happened to you and track the signs and progress as thoughts become things.

～ Be kind and accountable for all your actions. Adopt radical self-responsibility and find compassion for others as we are all connected on this planet trying to find our own truth.

Chapter Seven

Flow

"Let the tide carry you when
you can't escape it."

~ Esther Williams

am probably not alone in confessing that I was recently struck by the absurdity of what could be called the spectacle of the billionaires' race to space during the pandemic. It was a time in recent history when Jeff Bezos, Elon Musk, and Richard Branson all seemed to be clamoring in tone deaf fashion to be the first passenger(s) to orbit our planet for a few minutes of glory and history-making. For those of us left on the ground (they did ask me to join them, but I declined as I was busy writing this book), it looked more like an ego-driven attempt to be the first non-NASA employee in space. One could hardly be faulted for thinking, "Hey, why don't you guys combine your salaries and work together to focus on some of the more burning issues back here on earth? Like ending world hunger, endemic poverty, and inequality?" But those spaceships are big shiny objects, so the plea was ignored.

Now don't get me wrong, I am a full supporter of progress in science, innovation, and I am also a big fan of planet Earth. I would like our species to be able to keep living here for as long as humanly possible. My point is, there is plenty to do here on earth. It starts with each of us – in our own backyard, garden patch, patio, yoga mat, easy chair, or wherever your favorite place might be to reflect on your life. I have presented a lot of ideas in this book, some of them my own, many from the great thinkers and doers of our time that have inspired me, so there has been a lot to take in. This intent was by design because for a long time I have been looking for a book to read that is a compilation of ideas about balance in life and work to learn from. When I couldn't find that book, I decided to write it. Take what you find interesting and explore it further, then leave behind what doesn't resonate with you.

Here is another idea that may help you propel your learning of some of these new ideas, or any ideas or concepts you want to learn in the future. It is called the Feynman Technique and is a method of learning developed by physicist Richard Feynman. This process helps unleash your potential and encourages you to develop a much deeper understanding of the thing you are studying. Feynman was a Nobel prize winning physicist who lived from 1918-1988 and he was famous not just for his work in physics, but for being able to explain high level, complicated subjects in very simple terms. These are the four key ingredients of the Feynman Technique:

1. Choose a concept you want to learn about
2. Explain it to a 12-year-old
3. Reflect, Refine, and Simplify
4. Organize and Review[53]

You can apply this technique to anything under the sun, better yet: make a game of it. I mentioned early on that I love to play games! Anyway, presuming you would like to learn more about some of the concepts presented in this book, follow this method for taking a deeper dive. In the first step, you decide on your topic, get a sheet of paper, and write down everything you know about the subject as if you were going to teach it to a child. As you gather more information and learn more about the subject, add to the sheet, maybe even use a different color pen - oooh, fancy. This way you can see your knowledge grow.

---

[53] *The Feynman Technique: The Best Way to Learn Anything.* (n.d.). https://fs.blog/feynman-technique/

Once you are certain you have a good understanding of the topic move on to step two.

The second step involves finding a 12-year-old and explaining it to them. Preferably one you know. Borrow a friend's if you don't have your own handy around the house. Be sure you are using simple words to explain – avoid jargon at all costs. It's not because you should be talking down to this young person, but because jargon is only a veil for true comprehension. It gets in the way of the essence of things. This dovetails nicely with the elevator pitch test we so often hear, "Can you explain what your job is to your 95-year-old grandma?"

The third step is refining, revising, and simplifying. How simply you can convey this subject will reflect the measure of your own understanding, which is why it is such a great exercise. You might try reading your explanation aloud before sharing with this willing child who has so graciously agreed to grant you a few minutes away from his Xbox. If you find you are using too many complicated words, or jargon, refine it again before you begin explaining it to him. Review your original material as many times as necessary until you have distilled it down to a simple explanation - just like an elevator pitch.

In the fourth step, you test drive your understanding out in the world by trying out your explanation on someone else. What questions do they ask you? Are they confused by anything you said? Take notes. Once you are satisfied you have successfully conveyed key learnings, save your notes somewhere that you can access real time. This way you can review what you learned any time and add to it if you want. Learning this technique not only helps your own understanding of things, but it also enables you not to be duped by others as well. The next time you hear someone explaining something in a complicated manner, using jargon, lingo, or technical terms, ask them to simplify it. If they can't, it means they don't really understand it as much as they may say they do.

I hope I have provided you with some new information that you can begin to explore to not only find balance in your life, but to discover new horizons, to test out innovations, to create the life you want to be living. In Mike Dooley's book *Manifesting Change: It Couldn't Be Easier;* he talks about the difference between dwelling from and dwelling upon the life you want to live. This means acting as if you are already living the life you want to be, rather than wistfully gazing upon that life from a distance. It is a bit of a Jedi mind trick, but we all played make believe as a child before we were too old to play it anymore and since life is 90 percent mental anyway, go ahead; what's the harm? According to Dooley, *dwelling from* is our ticket to a more harmonious, balanced life:

Dwelling from can be likened to…creating in your mind's eye the "mansion" of your wildest dreams—a mansion that's not just your home but a symbol for the full-blown life of your dreams. From this day forward, metaphorically, you are to gaze through its windows at the world outside, letting this view shape your behavior with regard to anything and every-one. Live your life from that outlook, the mind-set that says, "I *have* arrived; I *live* in abundance; I *have* new-found health and beauty, more friends, more laughter, and harmonious relation-ships." That's moving *into* your mansion, instead of remaining on the outside looking in.[54]

---

[54] Dooley. (2010). *Manifesting Change: It Couldn't Be Easier.*

I titled this chapter Flow because the concept of flow is something that we all, in some way, hope to achieve. We are all looking for some level of seamlessness in our lives with less struggle. The renowned creativity expert, researcher, and psychologist, Mihaly Csikszentmihalyi (pronounced chick-sent-mihally), coined the term *flow* as an ingredient to human well-being and happiness. It is the state we can find ourselves in when involved with a creative pursuit, or something else we love to do, where we lose all track of time and are fully immersed in the moment, like that state we easily inhabited as children when at play. He wrote, "The best moments in our lives are not the passive, receptive, relaxing times... The best moments usually occur if a person's body or mind is stretched to its limits in a voluntary effort to accomplish something difficult and worthwhile."[55]

While flow, according to the way that Csikszentmihalyi classified it, may not be directly related to balance in the way we have been discussing it, I believe that the more we seek out flow-like experiences in our lives, the more balanced we will feel. It is in our best interest to cultivate these experiences for ourselves, whether by pursuing our passions, exploring our proclivities, or testing our innovations and latest ideas. As discussed earlier, the more we stretch ourselves and are willing to risk failure and move outside of our comfort zone, the more we will discover our own resilience and creativity, enabling us to live a life of more meaning and fulfillment. It seems worth

55 *Mihaly Csikszentmihalyi.* (n.d.). https://www.pursuit-of-happiness .org/history-of-happiness/mihaly-csikszentmihalyi/?gclid=CjoKCQjw8p2 MBhCiARIsADDUFVHTL-D_gsa69m27WkBz2dt1EncycCY6Id2 JFwTe5JiuqBuY7c_uSSIaAt7aEALw_wcB

the risk, doesn't it?

Author Alan Seale, in his book *Transformational Presence: How To Make a Difference In a Rapidly Changing World*, a concept that we discussed back in Chapter 2, refers to flow in a slightly different but no less important way. He discusses the principles of "flowing" with the energy of what wants to happen, which is based upon a focused "connection" to that energy and your intuition, as opposed to forcing or pushing what you want to happen. Alan created three questions which he refers to as the "Transformational Presence Model" that you can ask yourself at any time and in any situation. The goal is to slow down long enough to observe how the flow of energy is functioning in your life, offer the energy the opportunity to show you what it wants to do, and see if you are helping or hindering its path. Sit quietly and ask yourself these questions aloud or in your mind one at a time with a long pause in between and see what surfaces. This process works when you are tapped into your intuition with an authentic and genuine intent:

1. What wants to happen in this current situation?
2. Who is it asking you to be or the role you play?
3. What is it asking you to do or the action step you need to take?[56]

Not only is this model simple to use, but I've also seen it work in countless scenarios personally, professionally, with my business clients, and when I teach. I am always amazed at the path or the answer that surfaces as a result, because

---

[56] Seale. (2017). *Transformational Presence: How to Make a Difference In a Rapidly Changing World.*

it is never obvious and absolutely creates the best outcome. Energy can be an amazing asset when it has the space to evolve and show you what wants to happen. Trust and listening to your intuition are the key.

As I finished my surf lessons, I thought about what I wanted to accomplish and what I really walked away with. Through the various challenges in and out of the water from balancing on top of the moving current to reading the breaks and anticipating timing, I realized that learning to surf was no different from any other new life skill a person tries to master in terms of the need to be present with yourself and your surroundings. The common thread across all our experiences both positive and negative is whether we decide to first show up and second be open to receive what the experience can teach. Some days are better than others to use that information. In the big scheme of things, everything we do defines who we are. If you wake up one morning and decide you no longer like the person you see in the mirror, the good news is you can make a choice at any time to reinvent yourself and your story using a growth mindset - no permission slip needed.

I hope you found this information useful and somewhere along the way you had a "Scooby" moment where you tilted your head and said, "huh?" That is an opportunity knocking on your door and a cause for pause to do some internal research. The key takeaway from this book is that living a life of connected balance is a healthy choice that can create success in business and in life. What you do with that choice is up to you as you are **never** trapped. Feeling trapped is an illusion based on fear that we all experience from time to time when we are not grounded in our truth. Always remember that fear is **not** real, it doesn't serve our best interests or support our goals, and it definitely holds us back from living our best life. I will close with my all-time favorite quote:

"Sing like no one's listening, love like you've never been hurt, dance like nobody's watching, and live like it's heaven on earth."

~ Mark Twain

Maybe I'll see you at the beach, I will be the one standing at the water's edge with my paddle in hand ready to take on the waves. Thanks for reading!

KEY TAKEAWAYS

〜 Choose a concept you are interested in and use the Feynman Technique to test your explanation out on someone. Call a good friend or your Mom, if you can: she would love to hear about it.

〜 What things in your life are you forcing instead of letting them flow? Identify 2-3 key areas that need focus and make a conscious choice to shift them.

〜 What key idea or thing do you want to "dwell from" where you can apply Mike Dooley's philosophy? Are you living inside or outside the mansion?

〜 Is there an area of your life that lacks clarity? Try using the three questions from Alan Seale's Transformational Presence Model to gain some new insight or information using a growth mindset.

〜 Identify any fears you have and the associated limiting beliefs that are attached to them. Examine why you believe both are real. Create an action plan to overcome them and move toward accomplishing your dreams or goals.

Connected Balance Resources

CHAPTER ONE | INCOHERENCE

∽ Schedule 15 minutes a day just to think by yourself. That's it. Nothing else. If you can get outside to do it, even better.

∽ Discover your "why" by doing some real soul searching, so you can understand what makes you tick. For help getting started, pick up a copy of Simon Sinek's book *Start with Why;* his podcasts can also be found at www.simonsinek.com.

∽ Identify 1-3 areas in your life you know are incoherent and out of alignment with who you really are and what you want. Focus on how you can shift those areas to a place that feels better.

∽ Take a personal inventory of your task list and remove a few things from your plate. Learn how to slow down, relax, and take a nap if you don't know how to already. There is great benefit to stillness.

～ Make a conscious decision to get more sleep and exercise regularly. The body repairs itself during deep sleep and exercise improves sleep quality, plus helps you fall asleep more quickly. Winner!

CHAPTER TWO | BALANCE

～ When you are feeling disconnected in your life, take time to reflect on where you might be out of balance to avoid your own version of the twisties. Take time out in nature to make your own mini-Thoreau-like retreat.

～ Become a transformational leader and inspire others to change expectations, perceptions, and motivations to work towards common goals as a team.

～ Embrace your Yin and Yang and appreciate both masculine and feminine qualities as we need a balance of both in each of us.

～ Look for patterns and inspiration in nature to draw analogies, create meaning or innovations in your own life like Biomimicry does.

～ Learn more about HeartMath tools to create coherence as the heart is as much a center of intelligence as the brain is, so give it due respect. www.heartmath.org

CHAPTER THREE | CONNECTION

∽ If you feel you are living according to other's expectations, take a step back and examine what you really want. Figuring this out is a first step in the right direction.

∽ Making a conscious choice to be happy in each moment is taking your power back from letting outside forces and other people define you. Happiness is an inside job and despite all our grooming to the contrary, it is something within our control and leads to a state of positive being.

∽ Focus on your strengths and what comes naturally to you, so you are living in a positive state of being. Trying to be good at everything is a recipe for spreading yourself too thin, not being kind to yourself, and not honoring your unique talents.

∽ Once you get used to the idea of just being, you will become more in touch with your feelings and intuition. This will create better clarity around what wants to happen, and you will be more comfortable taking that inspired action – meaning just following your intuition as ideas and feelings surface.

∽ Start to pay more attention to what just feels right and trust your gut hunches. The more you experience the positive feedback that follows, the more this becomes a positive feedback loop over time and your confidence in your instincts will grow. Use them.

CHAPTER FOUR | TRUST

∽ Question conventional wisdom and anything you assume to be true without analyzing it from a critical perspective. Confirm that truth to be your own.

∽ Define what trust means to you and why it's important to create better alignment within your business and life. Share this information with those that matter to you.

∽ Ask yourself if you feel you are being held back by societal expectations or caught up in a belief system that is not yours. If so, work to realign your thinking toward your core values.

∽ Examine your beliefs and see if they are aligned with what you really want to achieve and if they aren't, challenge yourself to think differently and evolve them without judgement.

∽ Spend time figuring out or confirming your core values, then apply them to your decision-making process where and when you can.

CHAPTER FIVE | FAILURE

∽ **Redefine failure.** Make a list of what went wrong in your most recent experience of failure and see what you can learn and tweak to try differently next time.

∽ **Share your failures.** Share stories at work about your own personal failures. Show people it's okay to try – and to fail. Leading by example will help others move forward after failure and learn from it.

∽ **Create a failure award.** Do this for yourself, for your family, for your team at work, and make it fun. Reward the courage to try something that didn't work, then discuss and learn from it.

∽ **Keep an open mind.** Shift your mindset to see mistakes as a teachable moment. Trial and error along with failure is the best teacher since hindsight is 20/20. This will help reframe perceived failures into a series of different and possible outcomes to learn from.

∽ Don't beat yourself up over past mistakes, learn from them then let them go. The more you are forgiving and kind to yourself, the more you will be present in the moment.

CHAPTER SIX | KARMA

∽ Identify what is really important to you and focus on it with fierce intent. Be brutally honest with yourself and don't let past failures or disappointments hijack your dreams.

∽ Focus on gratitude daily and getting into a regular practice of positive self-talk. Science has proven optimism leads to more positive outcomes, so keep your glass half full.

- Be mindful and intentional with your words. Communicate with others the way you hope to be communicated with as words are powerful and can't be taken back.

- Visualize success. See it as if it has already happened to you and track the signs and progress as thoughts become things.

- Be kind and accountable for all your actions. Adopt radical self-responsibility and find compassion for others as we are all connected on this planet trying to find our own truth.

CHAPTER SEVEN | FLOW

- Choose a concept you are interested in and use the Feynman Technique to test your explanation out on someone. Call a good friend or your Mom if you can, she would love to hear about it.

- What things in your life are you forcing instead of letting them flow? Identify 2-3 key areas that need focus and make a conscious choice to shift them.

- What key idea or thing do you want to "dwell from" where you can apply Mike Dooley's philosophy? Are you living inside or outside the mansion?

- Is there an area of your life that lacks clarity? Try using the three questions from Alan Seale's Transformational Presence Model to gain some new insight or information using a growth mindset.

∽ Identify any fears you have and the associated limiting beliefs that are attached to them. Examine why you believe both are real. Create an action plan to overcome them and move toward accomplishing your dreams or goals.

ANNUAL REVIEW QUESTIONS

1. What one thing did you spend the most time doing this year to connect to yourself for better alignment?

2. What did you learn from the world's events this year?

3. What did you learn about your inner self that you can now apply across your life?

4. What made you happiest and gave you the most joy?

5. What didn't work or was an epic failure and what did you learn?

6. What life goals did you accomplish?

7. What didn't you get to that you will continue to work on?

8. What dreams are you moving toward now and why?

Suggested Reading List

After the Fall: How Humpty Dumpty Got Back Up Again, Dan Santat

Breaking the Habit of Being Yourself: How to Lose Your Mind and Create a New One, Dr. Joe Dispenza

Built to Last: Successful Habits of Visionary Companies, Jim Collins & Jerry I. Porras

Change Your Questions Change Your Life: 10 Powerful Tools for Life and Work, Dr. Marilee Adams

Deep Work, Cal Newport

Give and Take: A Revolutionary Approach to Success, Adam Grant

GRIT: The Power of Passion and Perseverance, Angela Duckworth

Hardwiring Happiness, Dr. Rick Hanson

Humor Me: America's Funniest Humorists on the Power of Laughter, Anthology

Liminal Thinking: Create the Change You Want by Changing the Way You Think, Dave Gray

Manifesting Change: It Couldn't Be Easier, Mike Dooley

Miracles at Work: Turning Inner Guidance into Outer Influence, Emily Bennington

Radical Forgiveness, Colin Tipping

Start with Why: How Great Leaders Inspire Everyone to Take Action, Simon Sinek

Swimming Lessons: Life Lessons from the Pool, from Diving in to Treading Water, Penelope Niven

The Ascent of Humanity, Charles Eisenstein

The Choice: Embrace the Possible, Dr. Edith Eva Eger

The Four Agreements: A Practical Guide to Personal Freedom, Don Miguel Ruiz

The Missing Piece Meets the Big O, Shel Silverstein

The Power of Now, Eckhart Tolle

The Quantum Leap Strategy, Dr. Price Pritchett

The Universe Has Your Back, Gabrielle Bernstein

The Untethered Soul: The Journey Beyond Yourself, Michael A. Singer

Transformational Presence: How to Make A Difference In a Rapidly Changing World, Dr. Alan Seale

Unexpected Awakenings, Sharna Langlais

Walden, Henry David Thoreau

You²: A High-Velocity Formula for Multiplying your Personal Effectiveness in Quantum Leaps, Dr. Price Pritchett

You Are a Badass, Jen Sincero

References

Apstein, S. (2021, August 2). *Former Gymnasts Left Paralyzed Are No Stranger to the Struggles Biles Faced.* Sports Illustrated. https://www.si.com/olympics/2021/08/02/simone-biles-twisties -physical-risk-former-gymnasts-left-paralyzed

A Stoic Response to Failure. (n.d.). Daily Stoic. https://dailystoic.com/ stoic-response-failure/

Bass, B. (1999). *Two Decades of Research and Development in Trans- formational Leadership.* European Journal of Work and Organi- zational Psychology, 8:1, 9-32, DOI: 10.1080/135943299398410

Bernstein, G. (2016). *The Universe Has Your Back.* Carlsbad, Califor- nia: Hay House, Inc. ISBN: 9781401946548

Bernstein, L. (2019, April 30). *The Perfect Book to Refresh Your Out- look on Life.* Off the Shelf. https://offtheshelf.com/2019/04/ the-choice-by-edith-eva-eger/

Brooks, K. (2021, February 10). *9 million U.S. small businesses fear they won't survive pandemic.* CBS News. https://www.cbsnews. com/news/small-business-federal-aid-pandemic/

Burroughs, J. (n.d.). *Can Imagining Success Actually Help You Achieve It?* [Video File]. https://olympics.com/en/video/can -imagining-success-actually-help-you-achieve-it-olympic -state-of-mind?uxreference=playlist

Dartnell, A. (n.d.). *6 Benefits of Failure That Prove That It Is Actually a Good Thing.* Lifehack. https://www.lifehack.org/articles/work/

6-benefits-failure-that-proove-that-actually-good-thing.html

Dooley, M. (2010). *Manifesting Change: It Couldn't Be Easier*. Simon & Schuster. ISBN-13: 978-1582702766

Duckworth, A. (2016). *Grit: The Power of Passion and Perseverance*. Toronto: Collins, an imprint of HarperCollins Publishers. ISBN: 9781443442312

Duckworth, A. (2021). *FAQ*. Angela Duckworth. https://angeladuckworth.com/qa/#faq-63

Dweck, C. (2016, January 13). *What Having a "Growth Mindset" Actually Means*. Harvard Business Review. https://hbr.org/2016/01/what-having-a-growth-mindset-actually-means.

Dweck, C. (2016). *Mindset: The New Psychology of Success*. New York: Ballantine Books. ISBN: 9781400062751

Eisenstein, C. (2013). *The Ascent of Humanity: Civilization and the Human Sense of Self*. North Atlantic Books. ISBN-13: 978-1583945353

Episode 697: Alone Together. (2020, March 20). This American Life, transcript. https://www.thisamericanlife.org/697/transcript

Failure. (n.d.). In *Merriam-Webster online*. https://www.merriam-webster.com/dictionary/failure

The Feynman Technique: The Best Way to Learn Anything. (n.d.). fs blog. https://fs.blog/feynman-technique/

Florida, R. and Ozimek, A. (2021, March 5). *How Remote Work Is Reshaping America's Urban Geography*. The Wall Street Journal. https://www.wsj.com/articles/how-remote-work-is-reshaping-americas-urban-geography-11614960100

Frost, M. (2009). *The New Global Student: Skip the SAT, Save Thousands on Tuition, and Get a Truly International Education*. New York: Three Rivers Press. ISBN: 9780307450623

Gabriel, R. (2016, January 8). *How Does Karma Affect Your Life?* Chopra. https://chopra.com/articles/how-does-karma-affect-your-life

Gardner, H. (2011). *Theory of Multiple Intelligences*. Basic Books; 3rd Edition. ISBN-13: 978-0465024339

Gatto, J.T. (2017). Dumbing Us Down: The Hidden Curriculum of Compulsory Schooling. Gabriola Island, British Columbia: New

Society Publishers. ISBN: 9780865718562

Halbfass, W. (2000). *Karma und Wiedergeburt im indischen Denken.* Diederichs, München. Germany. ISBN-13: 978-3896313850

Hanson, R. (2013). *Hardwiring Happiness: The New Brain Science of Contentment, Calm, and Confidence.* Harmony. ISBN-13: 978-0385347334

Hargreaves, S. (2013, December 18). *The Myth of the American Dream.* CNN Business. https://money.cnn.com/2013/12/09/news/economy/america-economic-mobility/

Haqqi, T. (2020, January 29). *5 Biggest IPOs of 2020.* Insider Monkey. https://www.insidermonkey.com/blog/5-biggest-ipos-of-2020-916171/5/

HeartMath. (n.d.). https://www.heartmath.com

Herman, A. (2008). *Gandhi & Churchill: The Epic Rivalry that Destroyed an Empire and Forged Our Age.* Random House. ISBN-13: 978-0553383768

Herrling, S. (2015, November 17). *The Myth of the Entrepreneur.* The Case Foundation. https://casefoundation.org/blog/the-myth-of-the-entrepreneur/

Horgan, J. (2018, July 23). *David Bohm, Quantum Mechanics and Enlightenment.* Scientific American. https://blogs.scientificamerican.com/cross-check/david-bohm-quantum-mechanics-and-enlightenment/

Itani, O. (2021, March 12). *How Living by Your Personal Values Helps You Become More Intentional in Your Life Decisions.* Omar Itani. https://www.omaritani.com/blog/personal-values-and-intentional-living

Jung, C.G. (1969). *Synchronicity: An Acausal Connecting Principle.* Princeton, New Jersey: Princeton University Press. ISBN 978-0-691-15050-5

"Karma" in: John Bowker (1997), The Concise Oxford Dictionary of World Religions. Oxford University Press.

Loneliness and the Workplace. (2020). Cigna. https://www.cigna.com/static/www-cigna-com/docs/about-us/newsroom/studies-and-reports/combatting-loneliness/cigna-2020-loneliness-infographic.pdf

McCraty, R. (2018, May 9). *Why heart coherence is important to health & well-being* [Video]. YouTube. https://youtu.be/-szBnENCdXo

Meckler, L. and Natanson, H. (2020, December 6). *'A lost generation': Surge of research reveals students sliding backward, most vulnerable worst affected.* The Washington Post. https://www.washingtonpost.com/education/students-falling-behind/2020/12/06/88d7157a-3665-11eb-8d38-6aea1adb3839_story.html.

Method. (n.d.). North Light Coaching. https://www.northlightcoaching.com/method

Mihaly Csikszentmihalyi. (n.d.). The Pursuit of Happiness. https://www.pursuit-of-happiness.org/history-of-happiness/mihaly-csikszentmihalyi/?gclid=CjoKCQjw8p2MBhCiARIsADDUF VHTL-D_gsa69m27WkBz2dt1EncycCY6Id2JFwTe5JiuqBuY7c_uSSIaAt7aEALw_wcB

Mitchell, J.M., Bogenschutz, M., Lilienstein, A. et al. (2021, May 10). *MDMA-assisted therapy for severe PTSD: a randomized, double-blind, placebo-controlled phase 3 study.* Nature Medicine. https://www.nature.com/articles/s41591-021-01336-3.

Murray, R. (2014, November 17). *What it's like to be a professional cuddler.* abcNews. https://abcnews.go.com/US/professional-cuddler/story?id=26973763

Pritchett, Price. (n.d.). *You2.* Pritchett LP. https://www.pritchettnet.com/you2

Seale, A. (2017). *Transformational Presence: How To Make a Difference In a Rapidly Changing World.* Center for Transformational Presence. ISBN-13: 978-0982533024

Scobie, C. (2003, August 31). *Why now is bliss.* Telegraph Magazine. Retrieved from https://clairescobie.com/wp-content/uploads/2014/12/On-Guru-Eckhart-Tolle_Aug03.pdf

Shuster, E. (2020, August 3). *The World Needs More Female Investors.* CTech by Calcalist. https://www.calcalistech.com/ctech/articles/0,7340,L-3799491,00.html

Silverstein, S. (1981). *The Missing Piece Meets the Big O.* New York: Harper Collins. ISBN: 9780060256579

Sinek, S. (2011). *Start with Why: How Great Leaders Inspire Everyone to Take Action.* Portfolio. ISBN-13: 978-1591846444

Six Principles. (2021). Liminal Thinking. http://liminalthinking.com/six-principles/

Solomon, M. (2020, February 23). *How To Bring Ritz-Carlton Caliber Customer Service To Any Type Of Business.* Forbes. https://www.forbes.com/sites/micahsolomon/2020/02/23/how-to-bring-ritz-carlton-caliber-customer-service-to-any-type-of-business/?sh=74d545c7657d

State of Remote Work. (n.d.). Buffer. https://buffer.com/state-of-remote-work-2019

Taleb, N. (2010). *The Black Swan: The Impact of the Highly Improbable.* Random House Trade Paperbacks; 2nd ed. Edition. ISBN-13: 978-0812973815

Thoreau, H.D. (2017). *Walden: Life in the Woods.* Gibbs Smith. ISBN: 978-1423646792

U.S. Bureau of Labor Statistics. (n.d.) United States Department of Labor. https://www.bls.gov/

Vanderbilt, T. (2012, September). *How Biomimicry is Inspiring Human Innovation.* Smithsonian Magazine. https://www.smithsonianmag.com/science-nature/how-biomimicry-is-inspiring-human-innovation-17924040/

Welcome to our cuddle website! (n.d.). Die Kushel Kiste. https://cuddlers.net/en

Welsh, J. (2019, April 24). *20 Tech-For-Social-Good Startups To Watch As Tech Nation Tackles Signs Of The Sector Stalling.* Forbes. https://www.forbes.com/sites/johnwelsheurope/2019/04/24/20-tech-for-social-good-startups-to-watch-as-tech-nation-tackles-signs-of-the-sector-stalling/?sh=1892093b300b

Wheeler Wilcox, E. (n.d.). *Thoughts are Things.* Ella Wheeler Wilcox. http://www.ellawheelerwilcox.org/poems/ptthings.htm

Wright, D. and Netter, S. (2014, March 13). *Cuddling Babies: Hospital Volunteers Show the Power of Human Touch.* abc News. https://abcnews.go.com/blogs/headlines/2014/03/cuddling-babies-hospital-volunteers-show-the-power-of-human-touch/

References

Yips. (updated 2021, November 17). Wikipedia. https://en.wikipedia.org/wiki/Yips

Zucker, R. (2019, February 12). *Why Highly Efficient Leaders Fail.* Harvard Business Review. https://hbr.org/2019/02/why-highly-efficient-leaders-fail

www.ingramcontent.com/pod-product-compliance
Lightning Source LLC
Chambersburg PA
CBHW020357130626
46549CB00006B/2315